"Everywhere I go women are searching for discipleship tools, either for themselves or for those they are discipling. Katie Orr has delivered up a fresh, substantive tool to accomplish both. FOCUSed15 is a serious study method that is possible even for those with demanding responsibilities. This material will fit in a variety of settings and for women everywhere on their spiritual journey."
—KATHY FERGUSON LITTON, national consultant for ministry to pastors' wives, North American Mission Board

"Katie Orr brings a unique and productive method of studying Scripture to the world of Bible studies. I enthusiastically encourage women to explore this effective and enjoyable method of Bible study!"
—SUZIE HAWKINS, author and longtime member of Southern Baptist Convention Pastors' Wives, wife of O. S. Hawkins

"Katie Orr has designed devotional material for the busy woman in mind—a focused 15 minutes a day that leads the reader to encounter the biblical text with guidance that reinforces solid principles of biblical interpretation and helpful application that makes God's Word come alive in our daily choices."
—TREVIN WAX, managing editor of *The Gospel Project*, LifeWay Christian Resources

"Katie Orr has a passion for Scripture and for women to know Scripture. This passion shows in her FOCUSed15 Bible study method, which she uses to lead women through books of the Bible and topical doctrinal studies. She proves that inductive Bible study doesn't have to be complicated but can be deeply impactful and fruitful."
—CHRISTINE HOOVER, author of *From Good to Grace* and *The Church Planting Wife*

"FOCUSed15 gives women an opportunity to learn the tools of inductive Bible Study in bite-sized chunks. Perfect for anyone who is committed to studying the Word in this time-crunched culture!"
—ANDREA BUCZYNSKI, vice president of global leadership development/human resources for CRU

D0062420

"The Scriptures are like jewels. When you look from different angles they glimmer in beautiful and unexpected ways. FOCUSed15 gives a fresh way to examine and enjoy the most precious words on Earth. Katie Orr's zeal for God's Word is contagious and may forever change the way you engage the Bible."

—JESSE LANE, vice president of connections at Seed Company

"Katie Orr has both the unique ability to make deep, meaningful Bible study doable for others and the passion for helping women love God more through the study of His Word. Through her Bible studies, Katie teaches others how to methodically grasp and absorb biblical theology in digestible bite-sized chunks. Her distinct and approachable gift of leading others through Scripture gives those with a desire to dive into God's Word a wonderful opportunity to both understand and apply deep biblical truths in their everyday."

—CHRYSTAL EVANS HURST, coauthor *of Kingdom Woman*

"I believe weariness is a feeling, and hope is a choice to believe what God says is true really is true. But sometimes, when the storms of life hit, I forget to choose hope, and need someone to come alongside me to help me remember. In this beautiful Bible study, Katie Orr invites us into a deeper understanding of what God's Word has to say about the subject, and reconnects us with the heart of our Savior. There's nothing like diving into Scripture to give a girl hope, and Katie helps us make the leap."

—BROOKE MCGLOTHLIN, president and cofounder of Raising Boys Ministries, and coauthor of *Hope for the Weary Mom: Let God Meet You in the Mess*

EVERYDAY

hope

Holding Fast to
His Promise

KATIE ORR

Other books in the
FOCUSed15 Bible study series:

Everyday Faith:
Drawing Near to His Presence

Everyday Love:
Bearing Witness to His Purpose

FOCUSed
15
Bible
Study

EVERYDAY

Holding Fast to His Promise

KATIE ORR

NEW HOPE®
PUBLISHERS
Gospel-Centered. Missions-Driven.

BIRMINGHAM, ALABAMA

New Hope® Publishers
PO Box 12065
Birmingham, AL 35202-2065
NewHopePublishers.com
New Hope Publishers is a division of WMU®.

New Hope Publishers serves its authors as they express their views, which may not express the views of the publisher.

Library of Congress Control Number: 2015917316

Cover Design: Michelle Drashman
Interior Design: Glynese Northam

ISBN-10: 1-59669-462-9
ISBN-13: 978-1-59669-462-0

N164102 • 0116 • 2M1

Dedication

To my parents, who faithfully and sacrificially provided for me, you laid a family foundation of love, stability, and commitment from which I stand to lead. Thank you. I love you.

Contents

Introduction

*Blessed be the God and Father of our Lord Jesus Christ!
According to his great mercy, he has caused us to be born
again to a living hope.*

—1 PETER 1:3

I'M PARTICULARLY DRAWN to instructions. I long for someone to tell me what to do when in order to achieve my desired outcome. Whether it be how to put a savory, yet nutritious meal on the table in less than an hour cooking time, or the best way to maximize my time as a work-at-home mom, I'm especially drawn to the how-to's in the areas I feel weak.

I think many people are this way, and our spiritual life is no different. It only takes a quick stroll down the self-help book aisle to see what we all crave: something more than what we have now. It's easy to feel depleted and defeated emotionally, relationally, and spiritually.

As a Christian, the pressure's on to be a beacon of light to the lost world around me, yet sometimes I can't seem to shake the feeling I should be doing or experiencing something I'm not. Scripture tells us that Christ came to earth to provide a living hope (1 Peter 1:3). It's one thing to read these words on a paper and say, "Amen." However, it's quite another to experience this living hope in our everyday lives.

Maybe you feel this dissonance as well?

You and I are on a voyage. A journey toward this living hope and abundant life our Creator and Savior has promised. However, our travels can feel more like we're aimlessly tossing in a storming sea of hopelessness. If you hold this study in your hands, I assume it is because, on some level, you desire to find a way to hope better for the trip ahead. You may find yourself today looking for a way out of the chaos, for the ladder that will lead to the lifeboat that promises rescue from the storm. Or, maybe you've given up altogether, and all you have left is a weak cry for help from the bottom of the boat.

You may have heard from others: "Keep your chin up. Don't lose hope!" It's easy to hope as a verb—something we need to do. An action we need to take. Though there are actions we can and should take when our soul is in despair, trying to conjure up the strength to be hopeful is not helpful.

It's impossible.

> *Hope* is a noun, not a verb. It is not something we do to escape the storm. Hope is what we hold fast to, as we endure each wave.
>
> Hope is a treasured possession, not an action.
>
> Hope is a guiding light, not a ladder to climb.
>
> Hope is a steadfast anchor, not a search for more.
>
> Hope is a harbor of promise, not a way of escape.

Our hope is the gospel of Christ. The good news of Jesus is not a one-time experience; it's a moment-by-moment need. This study of hope is a study of this good news—our salvation by grace through faith—and the implications it brings into our everyday lives. I'm so glad you're on this journey with me.

—Katie

God, we are desperate to experience the hope of Christ in our everyday. We look forward in anticipation to all You have planned for us through Your Word. Open our eyes to see the truths the Bible holds about our gospel-hope. Soften our hearts to receive them. Enable our souls and minds to follow You in obedience as we respond to all You will speak to us.

The Need for FOCUS

IF THIS IS your first FOCUSed15 study, you'll want to carefully read through the following introduction and study method instructions. After that, I'll see you on Day 1!

It's hard to focus.

In a world filled with continual demands for my attention, I struggle to keep a train of thought. Tasks I need to do. Appointments I need to remember. Projects I need to complete.

Yeah, it's hard to focus.

Without a good focus for my days, I wander. I lack the ability to choose well and avoid the tyranny of the urgent. Without focus, days become a blur—tossed back and forth between the pressing and the enticing.

WHY FOCUS MATTERS

I felt pretty lost during my first attempts at spending time with God in the Bible. After a few weeks of wandering around the Psalms and flipping through the New Testament, I realized I had no clue what I was doing.

It felt like a pretty big waste of time.

I knew the Bible was full of life-changing truths and life-giving promises, but I needed to learn how to focus on the details to see all that Scripture held for me.

In the medical world, we depend on the microscope. Even with all the fancy machines that can give test results in seconds, the microscope has yet to become obsolete. Some things can only be discovered through the lens of the scope.

What looks like nothing to the naked eye is actually teeming with life-threatening bacteria. Even under the microscope they may not be seen at first glance. But with the smallest adjustment of the focus, the blurry cloud of the field in view is brought into focus and the finest details are revealed.

And those details matter.

You need a microscope to make a diagnosis, but the microscope itself doesn't make the discoveries. It takes a trained eye to distinguish between cells. The average person may be able to figure out how to use the microscope to find a cell and get it in focus, but without training, the beginner will not know the clinical significance of what is seen.

Similarly, when we approach God's Word, we must learn to focus on what we are seeing and develop a trained eye to know its significance.

READY FOR MORE

I grew up in a shallow Christian culture. Don't do drugs. Don't have sex. Don't tell lies. Read your Bible. Be a light—sold-out for Jesus. This was the sum of being a good Christian, or so I thought.

Now, I'm your typical firstborn list-checker, so the do's and don'ts worked for me . . . for a while. But as I got older and the temptations of the don'ts became more enticing, I began to wonder if this Christianity thing was worth it.

Is this really what people spend their lives chasing? Seems tiring—and ultimately worthless.

Yet, God was drawing my heart—I could undeniably feel it—but I knew I was missing something. I thought I'd check out this reading-the-

Bible thing. Sure, I had read a devotional or two and knew all the Bible stories, but I didn't feel I knew God Himself.

A bit nervous, I drove to the local bookstore to buy my first really nice Bible. I excitedly drove back home, and headed straight to my room, opened up my leather-bound beauty and began to read . . .

. . . and nothing happened.

I'm not quite sure what I was expecting, but it sure wasn't confusion and frustration. I decided to give it another try the next day and still heard nothing. I had no clue what I was reading.

In all my years of storing up the do's and don'ts in my how-to-be-a-good-Christian box, I never caught a *how* or *why*.

For years I stumbled through my black leather Bible with very little learned on the other side of it all. Yet, God was faithful to lead and speak, and I fully believe that He can and does speak to us through His Word, even if we are as clueless as I was.

However, I also believe that God's Word is meant to be a great catalyst in our growth, and as we pursue how to better know God through His Word, we will experience Him in deeper ways.

You and I need a healthy, rich diet of God's Word in order to grow. And as we read, study, and learn to digest the Bible, we move toward becoming more like Christ. When we pursue the nearness of God, the don'ts become lackluster compared to the life-giving promises of His Word.

A FOCUSed 15 MINUTES

Over time, I learned incredible Bible study tools that took my time with God in His Word to a deeper level. Yet, with each method, Bible study seemed to take more and more time. Certain seasons of life allow for a leisurely time in the Bible; my experience has proven that most of my days don't.

As much as I would love to find a comfy chair in my favorite local coffee shop and study God's Word for hours, it is just not often possible. I'm lucky if I can get a decent breakfast in every morning before my day starts rolling. Distractions and demands abound, and many days I have not even tried to study my Bible because I just didn't have what it would take, time-wise, to get much out of it.

Until I learned to focus.

Even the busiest Christians can learn to focus and train their eyes to discover the life-changing truths held in Scripture. No incredibly long "quiet times" or seminary degree required.

All it takes is a focused 15 minutes.

The method I will walk you through consists of 15 minutes, five days a week. We will focus on the same set of verses over the course of a week, and each day of that week we will look at the passage with a different lens to gather new insights along the way.

TWO ULTIMATE GOALS

My prayer for you as we dive into the Bible is two-fold. First, I want to work myself out of a job. I want you to walk away from this study a bit more confident in your ability to focus on the transformational truths of Scripture on your own.

Second, I hope you will encounter our God in a deep and meaningful way through these focused 15 minutes. The most important thing about us is what we believe about God, and my prayer is that you will more accurately understand the truths about who He is through your own study of Scripture. As you get to know our glorious God better and better each day, I think you'll see your actions and attitudes are forever changed—because of who He is.

WHAT YOU'LL NEED

A pen to record your study notes and a journal for additional notes and any bonus study work you choose to do.

A Bible. If you don't have one, I recommend investing in a good study Bible. Visit my resources page at KatieOrr.me for solid study Bible suggestions.

Both a Greek interlinear Bible and Greek lexicon. There are in-print and free online versions for both. Check out my resources page for links.

A FEW IMPORTANT NOTES

This is only one method. This approach is my attempt at distilling down how I enjoy spending time in His Word. There are other great methods I use from time to time. Take what you can from this method and use what works for you; make it your own.

Fifteen minutes is just the starting point. Some of us are in a stage of life where we'll take 15 minutes whenever we can get it. Others may be able to carve out more time. I will give you suggestions for how to shorten or lengthen the study as needed. I think you will find yourself looking up at the clock and realizing you've accomplished a lot in a short amount of time.

Using online study tools will be of great help. You can certainly do this study without getting online; however, you will expedite much of the processes through utilizing the powerful—and free—online tools I suggest throughout our time together. I totally get that being online while trying to connect with God has its distracting challenges. Do what works for you. There is no "right" way to do this study. The only way to "fail" is to stop meeting with God.

Resist the urge to consult commentaries and study Bible notes right away. I am thankful for all the resources we have at our fingertips, but oftentimes devotionals, study Bibles, and the latest, greatest Bible teacher can be a crutch that keeps us from learning how to walk intimately with God on our own. While I do believe there is only one true meaning of each verse, God has a personalized word to speak to each of us through this study. Receiving big news from a loved one in a deliberate and personalized way means so much more to us than receiving the news third-hand, and when the Holy Spirit reveals a message to our hearts through God's Word, it will be something we hold to much more closely than someone else's experience of God. If at the end of the week, you are still unsure of the meaning of the passage, you will have time to look through commentaries.

For a list of my favorite online and print resources, including Greek study tools, commentaries, cross-referencing tools, and study Bibles, check out my resources page at KatieOrr.me.

How to FOCUS

OVER THE NEXT four weeks we will study hope together using the FOCUSed15 study method. You may want to think of me as your Bible coach. I will point you to the goal, give you what you need and cheer you on—but you'll be the one doing the work.

The FOCUSed15 method may be different than other studies you've completed. We're focusing on quality, not quantity. The goal is not to see how quickly we can get through each verse, but how deeply we can go into each verse and find everything we can about God and the hope we have in Him. This is how we can go deeper, in as little as 15 minutes a day, by looking at the same passage over the course of several days, each day using a new lens to view it. We're not trying to get everything we can out of the passage the first time we sit in front of it. Instead, we'll come back to it again and again, peeling back each layer, 15 minutes at a time.

Here is where we're headed:

- Week 1—Hope Is My Treasure
- Week 2—Hope Is My Lighthouse: FOCUSing on Ephesians 1:15–22
- Week 3—Hope Is My Anchor: FOCUSing on Hebrews 6:17–20
- Week 4—Hope Is My Harbor: FOCUSing on Romans 5:1–5

THE FOCUS METHOD

For me, high school history homework typically consisted of answering a set of questions at the end of the chapter. I quickly found that the best use of my time was to take each question, one at a time, and skim through the chapter with the question in mind. So, if the question was about Constantine, I would read the chapter wearing my "Constantine Glasses." All I looked for were facts about Constantine.

Little did I know then, this "glasses" method would become my favorite way to study God's Word. The FOCUSed15 method is essentially changing to a new pair of glasses with each read, using a different focus than the read before. Together, we will study one passage for five days, each day using a different part of the FOCUS method.

- Day 1—Foundation: Enjoy Every Word
- Day 2—Observation: Look at the Details
- Day 3—Clarification: Uncover the Original Meaning
- Day 4—Utilization: Discover the Connections
- Day 5—Summation: Respond to God's Word

For each day in our study, I will guide you through a different lens of the FOCUS study method, designed to be completed in as little as 15 minutes a day. There are also bonus study ideas with every day, providing ways to spend more time and dig even deeper if you can. We'll also start each day in prayer, declaring our dependence on the Spirit of God to open the eyes of our hearts to the truths in God's Word.

FOUNDATION
Enjoy Every Word

Many of us are conditioned to read through Scripture quickly and are often left having no idea what we just read. So, to kick off our studies, we will write out our verses. Nothing too fancy, but an incredibly efficient way to slow down and pay attention to each word on the page.

OBSERVATION

Look at the Details

With our foundation work behind us, we'll spend the next day looking for truths in God's Word. This is a powerful use of our time; we cannot rightly apply the Bible to our lives if we do not accurately see what is there. Observation is simply noting what we see by asking ourselves "What is true here?" We're not yet trying to figure out what it means, we are simply beginning an assessment. I will guide you along the way as we look for specific truths like, "What does this passage say is true about my hope?" or "What is true about God in this passage?"

CLARIFICATION

Uncover the Original Meaning

This is going to be fun. We are going to look at the original language of the verses. Our three passages are in the New Testament, so we will be looking up the Greek. To do this we will follow three simple steps:

Step 1: DECIDE which English word to study.

In this step, we will look for any repeated or keywords to look up, then choose one to learn more about.

Step 2: DISCOVER the Greek word in an interlinear Bible.

Next, using an interlinear Bible, we'll find the original Greek word for the word we chose in Step 1.

Step 3: DEFINE the Greek word using a Greek lexicon.

Finally, we will learn about the full meaning of each Greek word using a Greek lexicon, which is very much like a dictionary.

We'll walk through an example together each week. You can also bookmark How to Do a Greek Word Study in the appendix for you to reference throughout the study.

UTILIZATION
Discover the Connections

> The infallible rule of interpretation of Scripture is the Scripture itself: and therefore, when there is a question about the true and full sense of any Scripture . . . it must be searched and known by other places that speak more clearly.
>
> —*The Westminster Confession of Faith*

Ever notice the little numbers and letters inserted in your study Bible? Most have them. The numbers are footnotes, helpful bits of information about the original text. The little letters are cross-references and important tools for study.

Cross-references are doing just that, referencing across the Bible where the word or phrase is used in other passages in the Bible. They may also refer to a historical event or prophecy significant to the verse you are studying.

Together, we will follow a few of the cross-references for each of our passages, as they will often lead us to a better understanding of the main teaching of our verses. If your Bible doesn't have cross-references, no worries! I will provide verses for you to look up, and refer you to online tools for bonus studies.

SUMMATION
Respond to God's Word

> A respectable acquaintance with the opinions of the
> giants of the past, might have saved many an erratic
> thinker from wild interpretations and outrageous
> inferences.
>
> —CHARLES SPURGEON

This is when we begin to answer the question, "How should this passage affect me?" To do this we will do three things:

1. IDENTIFY—Find the main idea of the passage.
With a robust study of our passage accomplished, we can now do the work of interpretation. Interpretation is simply figuring out what it all means. This is oftentimes difficult to do. However, if we keep in mind the context and make good observations of the text, a solid interpretation will typically result.

This day is when we will finally consult our study Bibles and commentaries! Commentaries are invaluable tools when interpreting Scripture. They are available on the entire Bible, as well as volumes on just one book of the Bible. For a list of free online commentaries, as well as in-print investments, check out KatieOrr.me/Resources.

2. MODIFY—Evaluate my beliefs in light of the main idea.
Once we have figured out what the passage means, we can now apply the passage to our lives. Many tend to look at application as simply finding something to change in their actions. Much in the Bible will certainly

lead us to lifestyle changes, but there is another category of application that we often miss: what we believe.

We must learn to see the character of God in what we study and ask ourselves how our view of Him lines up with what we see. Of course it is helpful to look for do's and don'ts to follow, but without an ever-growing knowledge of who God is, the commands become burdensome.

3. GLORIFY—Align my life to reflect the truth of God's Word.
When we see God for the glorious, grace-filled Savior He is, the natural response is worship; the do's and don'ts become a joy as they become a way to honor the One we love with our lives. Worship is true application.

ALL OF THIS . . . IN 15 MINUTES?!

Yes, I know this seems like a lot of ground to cover. Don't worry! I will be here to walk you through each day. Remember, instead of trying to go as fast as we can through a passage, we are going to take it slow and intentional. We'll look at one passage for an entire week, and apply one part of the method to the passage each day.

THE CHEAT SHEET

At the end of most days' studies, I've included a "cheat sheet." While trying to complete a Bible study, I've often been paralyzed with wondering, "Am I doing this the right way?" The cheat sheet is there for you to use as a reference point. It is not a list of correct answers, however, and is meant instead to provide just a little bit of guidance here and there to let you know you are on the right track.

There are also several references in the appendix you may want to refer to throughout our time together. If you are new to Bible study, you might consider spending a day to read through the appendices before beginning your study. I hope those pages will be of great help to you.

A NOTE TO THE OVERWHELMED

Bible study is not a competition or something to achieve. It is a way of communicating with our magnificent God. If you have little time or mental capacity (I've been there, moms with little ones!), ignore the bonus study ideas and enjoy what you can. Keep moving through the study each day, and know that you have taken a step of obedience to meet with God in His Word. Other seasons of life will allow for longer, deeper study. For now, embrace these precious moments in the Word and remember that Jesus is your righteousness. When God looks at you— overwhelmed and burned-out though you are—He sees the faithful obedience and perfection of Christ on your behalf, and He is pleased. Rest in that today, weary one.

PREPARING TO **FOCUS**

Hope Is My Treasure

Hope Is My Treasure

PREPARING TO **FOCUS**

The kingdom of heaven is like treasure hidden in a field,
which a man found and covered up. Then in his joy he goes
and sells all that he has and buys that field.

—MATTHEW 13:44

IN THE MOVIE *Divergent*, Beatrice Prior learns to control her fears in order to control her environment. Beatrice (Tris for short) must undergo a clinical test of hallucinations—the results of which hold significant implications. Tris defeats her greatest terrors by telling herself what is true. Though everything in her screams, "Panic!" she successfully faces her fears through the hallucinations: a flock of attacking birds and then a near-drowning experience. She is able to escape her most dreaded situations by remembering her reality. These crows are not real. The water is not real. Instead of giving into fear—and losing hope—she overcame frightening and debilitating situations with truth.

"You will know the truth, and the truth will set you free" (John 8:32).

Though I've already been set free from sin, through the atoning death and powerful Resurrection of Christ, I've spent many moments living in bondage to hopelessness. For far too long, I wandered this earth as a "Christ follower" without really knowing the hope I had in the One I claimed to follow. I knew all the facts of the gospel—the good news about Jesus—and the implications of it for my eternal destiny, yet I wasn't experiencing the hope of Jesus' work on the Cross for my here and now.

This study of hope is essentially a study of the gospel. And until we come to see Christ and all He's done for us as our greatest treasure, we will experience hopelessness. The first step to experiencing hope in our everyday is to know for a fact you are saved from your sin. If you do, you have a hope that nothing—and no one—on this earth can take away.

The gospel of Christ is our hope. Hope is the gospel of Christ.

1. Take a moment to begin your study in prayer. Use the space below to journal a prayer, asking the Holy Spirit to open your eyes to the reality about hope. Commit these next four weeks of study to God. Ask Him for the grace and strength to hold fast to the truth about your hope in Christ.

Before we move into our inductive (verse-by-verse) study of our three passages on hope, we need to get a better picture of what hope is, so we can cling to that hope. To start our journey toward a better understanding of hope, let's read a few verses while asking the question, "What is true about hope?"

2. Start first with Ephesians 2:12. What do you learn about hope from this verse?

3. Next, look up 1 Peter 1:3 and list below what it teaches about our hope.

4. Move on to Romans 15:4 and make your notes about hope.

5. Lastly, let's dive into Colossians 1:3–5, from another Letter of Paul to a group of believers. Look for our word *hope* as you read, and then note what you learn about hope to add to our growing list.

Salvation is often thought of as a one-time action. Certainly, we each come to a point—a beginning place—where we make the choice to place our faith in Christ as our only hope for a relationship with God. It's then we become "saved." However, this specific step we take to enter into God's work of salvation is only one piece of a much larger puzzle. Our salvation does not start and finish with a prayer of surrender. In fact, God has been working to save us before this earth was even created (Titus 1:2). This initial moment, where we recognize our need for Jesus and by faith accept the great and glorious grace God gives us, is only the beginning of our journey toward experiencing God's full and complete plan that He set into motion long ago.

SALVATION		
JUSTIFICATION	SANCTIFICATION	GLORIFICATION
Foundational Position	Refining Process	Final Perfection
DEATH · BY GRACE · LIFE / THROUGH **FAITH** / NO HOPE · WORK OF CHRIST · HOPE	HOLD FAST / **HOPE**	Harbor Of God's Presence for Eternity
in a moment	over a lifetime	for eternity

The Bible portrays three distinct parts of our salvation: justification, sanctification, and glorification, as depicted above in our diagram. These three fancy words are crucial to our understanding of gospel hope. Justification occurs when we come to a saving faith in Jesus and is a legal act in which God declares sinners righteous on the basis of Christ's righteousness. This "legal act" gives us a new place to stand before God, a platform of mercy and acceptance from which we can never be moved, and it is from this position of forgiveness and grace we walk forward in newness of life (Romans 6:4). Though sufficient in itself to bring us into relationship with our holy God, justification is simply the beginning of our salvation. From this moment of salvation, we enter the road of sanctification—the continual refining process of becoming more and more like Jesus. This sanctifying journey was initiated, is sustained, and will one day be completed by God (Philippians 1:6), yet our spiritual growth is either hindered or accelerated by our everyday actions. This sanctification process, in part, is why we are given so many commands throughout Scripture. As we abide in Christ (John 15:4), keep in step with the Spirit (Galatians 5:16–25), cling to the Word of God (Joshua 1:8), and become doers of all we learn (James 1:22), we are slowly transformed into the image of our Savior (Romans 8:29). Until one day we reach our final destination in heaven where our salvation will be complete and glorification will occur—our final perfection into the image of Jesus.

If you are in Christ, you have received hope (justification), you are receiving hope (sanctification), and you will receive hope (glorification), and we see all three in the verses we looked up today. I had no hope (Ephesians 2:12); I was given hope when God brought me from spiritual death to a new life (1 Peter 1:3); I can experience hope now through God's Word (Romans 15:4); and I have the ultimate hope of eternal life with God who awaits me in heaven (Colossians 1:5).

As we continue to learn and internalize all that is true about the gospel, and its implications on our everyday moments, we can experience the hope Jesus came to this earth to give. We can better hold fast to hope when we know better what it is we are clinging to.

God, I praise You for the hope You have given me through new life with Christ. I am so thankful for the justification I've experienced through the work of Christ on my behalf. Give me the grace to cling to You as I walk the everyday journey of

*sanctification, as You make me more and more like
Christ. I look forward to the hope I have waiting for me—
Your eternal and glorious presence.*

⸱!⸱ BONUS STUDY ⸱!⸱

Spend some time writing one or all of the verses we studied today. As
you write, ask God to penetrate your heart with the truths on the page.
Consider writing them out on 3x5 cards and posting them around your
house as a reminder of the hope you possess.

CHEAT SHEET

2. Start first with Ephesians 2:12. What do you learn about hope from this verse?

Before Christ, I had no hope; I was without God, separated from Christ, alienated from the family of God, strangers to God's covenant of promise.

3. Next look up 1 Peter 1:3 and list what it teaches about our hope.

• My hope is living.

• God caused me to be born again to this living hope.

• This hope was given to me through the Resurrection of Jesus.

4. Move on to Romans 15:4 and make your notes about hope.

• I can have hope.

• This hope is through endurance.

• This hope is through the encouragement of Scripture.

5. Lastly, let's dive into Colossians 1:3–5, from another Letter of Paul to a group of believers. Look for our word *hope* as you read, then note what you learn about hope to add to our growing list.

• Hope is laid up for me in heaven.

Hope Is My Treasure Because It's a Gift

PREPARING TO FOCUS

"This woman knows she's a sinner," Jesus told them. "She knows she'll never be good enough. She knows she needs me to rescue her. That's why she loves me so much. You look down on this woman because you don't look up to God. She is sinful on the outside—but you are sinful on the inside."

—*THE JESUS STORYBOOK BIBLE*

MOST WOULD SAY I was a pretty good kid. I achieved stellar grades and tried really hard to follow all the rules of society. I'm your typical firstborn type-A who desires a certain amount of respectability, so the fear of what my teachers, parents, and peers thought of me kept me out of quite a bit of trouble. I wanted people to look up to me and I think some did.

For a long time, I lived the "good" Christian life. I did the do's and I didn't do the don'ts. And because I jumped through those hoops, I figured I was a pretty good person. The reality is this: I was a pretty sheltered person. I'm thankful for the protection of my parent's choices and the guidance of my private school upbringing. They were God's provision of grace. However, if I had different parents, grown up in a different environment, even dated different (less-respectable) guys, I'm certain my sin nature would have had more opportunity to make a public appearance.

Truth is, my sin was incredibly evident (selfishness, disrespect, self-righteousness, and much more) but because they weren't the sins others considered "really bad," I thought I was OK. I viewed my life as a family room wall painted a pretty and pleasing shade of white, with a few dirty finger smudges of sin here and there. A few sassy words to my parents, a bit of gossip and envy, and a few moments of anger. Nothing a soapy rag, or a small touch-up of paint couldn't fix. This understanding of sin is far removed from the true depths of my disobedience and the unreachable heights of God's holiness.

God's hand of grace is not merely a hand that delivers. It's a hand that restrains. Some of you have a prodigal salvation story of complete and radical deliverance from sinful patterns; He's rescued you from drug abuse, sexual addictions, and a complete sprint away from anything associated with God. Though I've not walked down those specific sin paths, my soul is just as deeply stained by anger and coveting as the hearts of the addict and convict. The reality is, I'm not the pretty white wall I once thought I was. Before Christ, I lived in a crumbling structure I was attempting to hold up with loads of paint and pretty wallpaper. Underneath it all was a decaying, infested, crumbling soul in desperate need of a new blueprint.

> *Woe to you, scribes and Pharisees, hypocrites! For you are like whitewashed tombs, which outwardly appear beautiful, but within are full of dead people's bones and all uncleanness.*
>
> —MATTHEW 23:27

1. Spend some time thinking about your life before Christ. If you became a Christian as a young child, imagine how your journey would be different without the hope of Christ in your life. Journal a prayer of praise for the gift of

hope through justification (the fact that you stand righteous in the eyes of God today).

2. Read Titus 3:4–7 and fill out the chart below with the actions and character of God you see in this passage.

THE ACTIONS OF GOD	THE CHARACTER OF GOD

3. Take another look at Ephesians 2:12, which we looked at yesterday, and fill in the chart below with the truths about us before God intervened in our life.

TRUTHS ABOUT ME BEFORE CHRIST

The Bible has even more to say about the condition of our hearts without the grace and mercy of God. We are wretched, wicked sinners, you and I (Romans 3:23), and it's all too easy to get caught up in believing that behavior modification will affect our eternal destiny. There is no amount of whitewashing that can take away our stains. Our sin runs deep. And though we may try to cover it up with good deeds, our hearts are wicked. And wicked hearts cannot be in the presence of God.

But God, in His great mercy, sent Jesus to make the payment my sin debt owed. He took on my dilapidated, decaying mess and gave me . . . hope. He appeared. He saved. He poured out richly. He justified. He made. The gospel is a work of God. My only part is faith, of drawing near to Him, my only hope.

> *God, I praise You for saving me! You are good. You are full of love. You are my Savior. Your mercy and grace toward me is a great, great gift. Thank you for pouring out Your Holy Spirit on me. Help me to walk in the newness of life You have provided for me. Help me hold fast to this hope.*

⁘ BONUS STUDY ⁘

If you are familiar with the FOCUSed15 method, or would like to try it out a bit early, continue to FOCUS on Titus 3:4–7. We've already done some "observation" work on it. Feel free to refer back to the study method section.

FOUNDATION—Write out the verse.

OBSERVATION—In addition to the observation work you've already done, make a list of all this passage teaches about hope.

CLARIFICATION—Select a word or two to look up and find the original Greek meaning.

- Decide which English word to study.
- Discover the Greek word in an interlinear Bible.
- Define that Greek word using a Greek lexicon.

UTILIZATION—Follow any cross-references available.

SUMMATION—Journal through the following questions.

- Identify: What do you think the main idea of this passage is, in regard to hope? Consult a commentary to confirm your conclusion.
- Modify: How do your beliefs line up with the truths you've learned today?
- Glorify: How can you adjust your attitudes and actions to best glorify God with the truths of this passage?

CHEAT SHEET

2. Read Titus 3:4–7 and fill out the chart below with the actions and character of God you see in this passage.

THE ACTIONS OF GOD	THE CHARACTER OF GOD
Appeared	Goodness
Saved me by the washing of regeneration and renewal of the Holy Spirit	Loving kindness
	Our Savior
Poured out the Holy Spirit on me richly through Jesus Christ	Mercy
Justified me	Grace
Made me an heir of hope of eternal life	

3. Take another look at Ephesians 2:12, which we looked at yesterday, and fill in the chart below with the truths about us before God intervened in our life.

TRUTHS ABOUT ME BEFORE CHRIST
Separated
Alienated
Strangers
Having no hope
Without God

Hope Is My Treasure Because It Changes Me

PREPARING TO FOCUS

IT WAS NEW Year's Eve 2004, and a wave of nausea hit me like a ton of bricks. Technically, it was already January 1, 2005, as it was 2 a.m., and I couldn't keep my eyes open any longer. As a staff member working with Campus Crusade for Christ, late night discussions with college students were typical. However, this particular night left me physically exhausted. The nausea lingered throughout the next day, and I spent the day waiting for (what I thought was) the inevitable wave of vomiting to ensue. But it never came . . . and the nausea stuck around for several months.

Yep, you guessed it, I was pregnant. My husband and I were thrilled by the news, and so began our journey as parents. Pregnancy typically brings about a great excitement for the future, especially for first-time parents. Almost immediately, Chris and I began to imagine life with our little one. Life had forever changed. From the moment of seeing that positive pregnancy test, we lived life expectant.

In Day 1, you and I chatted about the process of our salvation: justification, sanctification, and glorification. Through a saving faith in Christ Jesus, we each had a moment when everything changed in the spiritual realm. Once lost, we were found. Though we were orphans, marked by disobedience and sin, we were chosen and adopted by God. A bunch of guilty sinners, now reconciled (brought back) and justified (made right).

Yet there is something about this that doesn't quite fit in my day-to-day experience. Instead of feeling found and forgiven, there are many moments when I feel lost, lonely, and extremely guilty because of my poor choices. I have been delivered from the penalty of sin . . . yet sinful patterns remain. I am righteous before God . . . yet my actions often demonstrate a different reality. There is a big difference between my position before God, and the current reality that faces me in the mirror. Just like when I was pregnant with my firstborn. I was a mother . . . but not yet. I had my little boy with me . . . but not yet. And once it began, the waiting, yearning, ache to be a mother forever changed me.

And so it is with our salvation. We already have right standing with God and though we know all that will be true of us when we see Jesus face-to-face, there is much to yearn for now. Though I know that God sees me through the righteousness of Christ, and that there is no condemnation for those who are in Christ Jesus (Romans 8:1), this soul is still incredibly stained. I am righteous . . . but not yet. And the longer I walk with Christ, the more I understand the depths of my sin. I hate my sin and I ache to be rid of it.

Holy. Complete. Forever.

These expectant days we live in are the age of sanctification—the process of becoming more and more like Jesus. And though the sinful flesh inside of me has been dealt a mortal wound by the power of Christ's death and Resurrection, it is not going down without a fight. It is dead . . . but not yet.

1. As we begin our study today, ask the Spirit of God to open your eyes to the truths in verses you will study today. Ask Him to give you a greater longing for His presence, and a greater disgust for your sin. Declare your need for His strength and power to overcome the sin that thrashes around within you.

2. Let's take a deeper look at Romans 15:4 from Day 1. Read it again, then write it out below. You might also try to outline or diagram the sentence, or even draw a picture to depict the verse. Do whatever helps you slow down and enjoy every word.

3. According to Romans 15:4, how are we able to experience hope?

4. Let's take a deeper look at how we can experience hope through endurance. Read Hebrews 12:1–2 in your Bible, and look for the commands in this verse. What are we told to do?

5. Romans 15:4 also states God's Word was written for our encouragement. I find Philippians 1:6 to be one of the most encouraging verses in the Bible. Read Philippians 1:6, then write it or draw it out below.

Here we see all three "stages" of our salvation. Paul, the writer of Philippians is stating that: (1) Jesus began a good work in us (justification). (2) He will bring it to completion at the day of Jesus Christ (glorification). (3) Just like Paul, we are to be "sure of this" (sanctification). Throughout the process of our sanctification, we are to hold fast to the hope that Christ has already done much for us and there is much more to come.

I am already saved by God—righteous before Him because of Jesus' death on the Cross—but I am not yet without sin. I already have hope, but my hope is not completely fulfilled.

Living in the "already . . . but not yet" days can be discouraging. I am a spotless saint, in God's view, because of what Christ has done for me on the Cross. But at present, until heaven, I am a stupendous sinner. Still, the process of sanctification gives me hope—a great and growing confidence in the One who will bring complete healing, full redemption, and His unhindered presence.

I am already saved . . . but not yet.

> *God, I praise You for Your Holy Scripture, which I can cling to in this great waiting room of life. Jesus, thank You for being my righteousness. Holy Spirit, bring comfort when my soul is weary. Father, be my strength when I am weak. Help me to*

*endure well as I wait for the fullness of Your presence
to be revealed.*

⸪ BONUS STUDY ⸪

Continue to FOCUS on any (or all) of the verses we looked at today. Follow the prompting of the Spirit as He leads and speaks through God's Word.

CHEAT SHEET

3. According to Romans 15:4, how are we able to experience hope?

• Through endurance

• Through the instruction and encouragement of Scripture

4. Let's take a deeper look at how we can experience hope through endurance. Read Hebrews 12:1–2 in your Bible, and look for the commands in this verse. What are we told to do?

• Lay aside any weight that hinders me.

• Lay aside my closely clinging sin.

• Run with endurance.

• Look to Jesus.

Hope Is My Treasure Because It Comes with a Promise

PREPARING TO **FOCUS**

*For in this hope we were saved. Now hope that is seen is not
hope. For who hopes for what he sees? But if we hope for
what we do not see, we wait for it with patience.*

—Romans 8:24–25

I'VE HAD SOME pretty amazing roommates. I went to Auburn University,
and each of my four years there can be defined by where I lived. Boyd
Hall. Thomaston Park. The Quad. Northpointe. Each name brings back
memories of friendships, football, and a newfound faith.

Through my childhood, I gathered a lot of information about God.
At first, in private Catholic schools, then later in Protestant Christian
schools, Bible was a subject . . . and I had straight A's. Later, as an awkward
yet outgoing middle school girl, I began to go to church on my own, and
the journey of my faith in God began. I vividly remember the moment I
first cried out to God for salvation. I knew all the right answers. I could
tell you about the gospel—about the hope you can find in Jesus—but I
hadn't really experienced it for myself. Until that late afternoon on my
hunter green and burgundy paisley comforter, where I first recognized
my true need for Jesus. I wasn't listening to a sermon, or reading my
Bible. It was just a normal day. I was piddling around in my room doing a
whole lot of nothing, and God showed up. The Holy Spirit convicted me

then and there and in an instant the blinders surrounding my heart were lifted and I could finally see my desperate need for Jesus.

My journey from there was a slow crawl, as I fumbled through my teen years trying to figure out what God wanted from me. So, I did the "do's" and I tried my best to stay away from the "don'ts." Fast-forward to the Boyd Hall era, my freshman year at Auburn, when I began to learn the "how's" and the "why's" of my faith in God, and I met girls who talked about Jesus like He was a real person—someone they knew intimately and loved dearly. It was then I knew I was missing out, and God began to lovingly show me that Christianity was not a list to be followed, but a relationship to be pursued. Having faith in God was not something to be achieved, but was a presence to draw near to.

On to my Northpointe days, my senior year. It was 2000; a new century had begun, and a season of intense and deep spiritual growth was coming to a close. My roommate Jill and I sat chatting in her bedroom. I can't quite recall what we were chatting about, but I do remember one thing: a dear friend (the one who had already walked through cancer at the age of 20) stating, "I can't wait for heaven!" The look on my face probably betrayed me, but I tried to act as if I shared her longing for all that is to come. But I didn't. Heaven was (and still is) hard for me to imagine. Earth, along with the people and things I loved on it, were (and still are) something I was not ready to let go of. I hoped for much: a successful career, a loving husband, a beautiful family, and a life spent enjoying all this world had to offer. But I didn't really hope for heaven.

As I sit here today, 15 years later, I still don't hope for heaven as I should. My soul is too easily satisfied with the temporary and trivial. Yet looking back, I can see the journey God has provided for me to walk. I have the career, the man, and the kids I wanted, but also a perspective to go with it all. I've learned they are gifts, wonderful and precious to me, but they cannot be my hope. They were never meant to be my hope. Because even the most faithful, godly man can disappoint; the most beautiful children can be ugly; the most successful career can dishearten.

"If in Christ we have hope in this life only, we are of all people most to be pitied" (1 Corinthians 15:19).

1. Ask God to reveal the place where you are holding on to something other than Him and the hope He gives through Christ. Journal through these places, and call out to the Holy Spirit for the grace and strength to move your grip from the temporary to the eternal.

2. Read Colossians 1:3–5 and write it out below.

Paul refers here to the gospel, and the hope laid up for us in heaven. Part of my disconnect with not longing for heaven was not understanding all that awaits me there. I am still on the journey toward better knowing all that heaven holds. Maybe you are, too?

Today we'll try out a new part of our FOCUS method, "utilization." For our utilization work, we can use cross-references, Bible dictionaries, or Bible concordances to see how certain words or phrases are used in other places in the Bible. I've listed several cross-references for you to look up, regarding what is laid up in heaven for those who know Jesus.

3. Read each verse and fill out the chart below with what the Bible has to say about what we can hope for in heaven. (This is not meant to be a comprehensive study of heaven. These are only the highlights!)

REFERENCE	WHAT I CAN HOPE FOR
Romans 6:23	
Romans 8:23	
1 John 3:2	
Revelation 21:3–4	

Hope is indeed a great and glorious treasure. Because of Christ, there is oh-so-much to look forward to in heaven! We have a great inheritance to look forward to. We will have eternal life in perfect bodies. There will be no sadness, pain, or sickness. And because we will have the righteousness of Christ, and in every way be like Him, we will be able to be in the presence of our Holy Heavenly Father, whom we will dwell with forever and ever.

"And night will be no more. They will need no light of lamp or sun, for the Lord God will be their light, and they will reign forever and ever" (Revelation 22:5).

God, show me where my heart is holding on to the promises of this world. Holy Spirit, enable me to let go of my grip on that which can never fulfill. Hold me by Your grace, as I hold on to the hope of all You have waiting for me. Open my eyes to the truths in Your Word about the hope You've given me through Christ.

⸫ BONUS STUDY ⸫

Look up these additional verses on all we have to look forward to in heaven.

REFERENCE	WHAT I CAN HOPE FOR
1 Peter 1:4	
Galatians 5:5	
2 Timothy 4:8	

CHEAT SHEET

3. Read each verse and fill out the chart below with what the Bible has to say about what we can hope for in heaven.

REFERENCE	WHAT I CAN HOPE FOR
Romans 6:23	Eternal life in Christ Jesus our Lord
Romans 8:23	• Adopted into the family of God • The redemption of my body
1 John 3:2	• I will be like Christ • I will see Christ as He is
Revelation 21:3–4	• God will dwell with me • I will be His people • God Himself will be with me as my God • He will wipe away every tear from my eyes • No death • No mourning • No crying • No pain • Former things have passed away

BONUS STUDY CHEAT SHEET

Look up these additional verses on all we have to look forward to in heaven.

REFERENCE	WHAT I CAN HOPE FOR
1 Peter 1:4	An inheritance that is: • Imperishable • Undefiled • Unfading • Kept in heaven for me
Galatians 5:5	The hope of righteousness
2 Timothy 4:8	The crown of righteousness for those who have loved God's appearing

Hope Is My Treasure

PREPARING TO **FOCUS**

I'M NOT MUCH of an actress, but much to my surprise, I landed a fairly big role in a musical put on by my high school. I assure you, the pickin's were slim. We had several performances, but to this day, one night stands out more than the others, and it isn't because of my stellar performance. During one of my dialogues, I stated a line that was out of place. I didn't even catch it or realize it until the very end of the play when my friend Amy walked up to me, and she didn't look happy.

You see, my misplaced line cued the rest of the cast to skip over several scenes, one of which included her big solo. It also happened to be the one performance the majority of her family had paid to come and see. Amy was sad, disappointed, and I'm sure angry, though I could tell she was trying her best to be gracious. I felt horrible. Yet—in true teenage form—I was too prideful to take full responsibility. I muttered a pathetic apology and attempted to shift blame to the rest of the cast who could have ignored my mistake and kept us on track, but I'm sure she saw right through my counterfeit sorrow.

That is one night I wish I could declare a do over. If I could go back, I would be more careful to speak the correct lines, and I would most certainly be more apologetic and sympathetic to my friend's frustration with me. My life contains numerous days and nights where I wish I could declare a do over. Unfortunately, many of those days hold more significant consequences and guilt than a simple slip of lines. They are filled with choices more hurtful and actions more reprehensible.

Though I can't go back and change the course of that theatric evening, God has given me the ultimate do over. Through Christ, I am given new birth that brought forth a completely new identity and a new ability to choose right. Because God knew that a simple do over wouldn't work. Had I been given another chance to do things right, I would choose pride and selfishness all over again. As I do every day. A new chance to do the right thing is not the answer I need.

Only a right person can make right choices, which is why the gospel is so glorious. It is only through Christ's righteousness, imparted to me through spiritual rebirth, do I now have the ability to choose well. Before Christ, I had no hope but to sin. Now, through faith in the redeeming work of Jesus, I possess a treasure—a hope—greater than anything this world can attempt to promise.

Today, let's take some time to slow down and digest what we've been learning by going through our application steps. Remember, this is when we begin to answer the question, "How should what I've learned affect me?" To do this we will do three things:

1. IDENTIFY: Find the main idea of each passage.

2. MODIFY: Evaluate my beliefs in light of the main idea.

3. GLORIFY: Align my life to reflect the truth of God's Word.

Take a deep breath in and ask the Holy Spirit to fill your heart today as you reflect on all you've learned this week. If your soul is anything like mine today, it is tired and in desperate need for a fresh wind of His movement and power.

STEP 1: IDENTIFY

1. Today, begin to process all you've learned by journaling through it. To start, fill out the chart below with the three stages of our salvation. Next, flip back to each day's study to review what you've learned, then add those truths to the appropriate section.

STAGE 1	STAGE 2	STAGE 3

STEP 2: MODIFY

2. How does my view of salvation line up with what I've learned this week?

3. Am I experiencing the treasure of living hope I was reborn to? If not, what is keeping me from truly knowing the hope of the gospel in my life?

4. How is my understanding of the true depths of my disobedi-ence and the heights of God's holiness?

5. How does knowing that I live in the "already . . . but not yet" days help me understand my journey of experiencing hope?

STEP 3: GLORIFY

6. What adjustments can I make to glorify God in my attitudes and actions today?

I am not commanded to have hope as though it was an item on my to-do list. Instead, I am to "hold fast" to the hope God has already provided (Hebrews 6:18). In order to obey this command to "hold fast," I must regularly take a good, hearty look at the hope I have in Christ. It is from this point of view, standing on the foundation of God's grace and with a firm belief that I am justified before Him, that I can hold fast to my treasured hope.

The gospel is my everything. My only hope.

God, help me to continually cling to Your grace. Through Christ alone I have a living, heavenly hope. For that I am eternally grateful.

FOCUSING ON **EPHESIANS 1:15–22**

Hope Is My Lighthouse

Foundation

FOCUSing ON EPHESIANS 1:15–22

*Why are you cast down, O my soul, and why are you in tur-
moil within me? Hope in God; for I shall again praise him, my
salvation and my God.*

—Psalm 42:5

DURING A DIFFICULT season of transition I found myself in a dark place.
I'd had one of those days, and the minute my husband took step into the
house, I made a beeline for the car. And I went. I had no destination, just
anywhere but the house. I needed to get out, clear my mind, and just drive.

My hand gripped the gray steering wheel as I made completely random
turns around that flat Florida town. It was almost dusk, and I chased the
sun in hopes it would shed some light on all the confusion and darkness
swirling around my heart and mind. I drove that blue minivan for aimless
miles, sobbing, yet for no specific reason beyond that I was just not happy.
Things with God were good. Things with Chris (my husband) were good.
Things with my (then two) little ones were crazy and hectic, but good.

But my soul wasn't good.

I followed a small country road out to nowhere, and as I approached
a set of train tracks a moment happened—a thought transpired—which
made the sobbing cease for just a moment. The thought sideswiped me as
if it was an unstoppable train on the tracks I was crossing:

*Just hit me. Just come down these tracks and take me away. I can't do this
anymore. I just want to be gone.*

The gravity of this thought frightened me more than anything had before, nor has since. I wanted to be dead. I wanted to leave this earth. I wanted a train to materialize out of thin air and kill me in an instant. And before you go thinking it was because I wanted to leave this earth to be with Jesus, He was not part of this train of thought.

I didn't recognize it as such then, but looking back I can see it oh-so-clearly now. I was depressed and struggling to experience the hope of the gospel. I knew it all in my head, but it wasn't penetrating my heart. Turns out, I had a hormonal imbalance and have since been successfully treated for depression. I continue to make lifestyle changes to keep up my mental health; however, even with the clinical depression at bay, I've had thousands of moments of hopelessness since then, in varying degrees (even some today!), as I continue to learn how to apply the glorious truth about Jesus to my everyday living.

So, if you are feeling hopeless today, or you did yesterday, or you do tomorrow . . . you are certainly not alone.

1. Open your time today in with an honest assessment of your experience of hope over the last several weeks. Rate your experience from 0 to 10. Spend some time in honest conversation with God about where you are. Whether you are at 10 or 0, praise God for the hope He has given you, and ask Him to shine the hope of the gospel into your dark places.

ENJOY EVERY WORD

This week we'll dive into Ephesians 1:15–21 to see clues this passage can give us to what keeps us from experiencing hope in our every moment.

Paul's prayer here in Ephesians 1 provides a clue to why we don't always experience the hope of the gospel. Remember, *hope* is a noun. It is something we possess; a gift we are given when we become an heir of Christ. It cannot be lost or taken away from us; however, our experience of this hope can be robbed. Paul prayed that the faithful would know their hope. So, they must have strayed from what they already knew and/ or their knowledge of the hope they had was somehow limited.

2. Today, we'll work through our first layer of studying Ephesians 1:15–21 by writing the passage. This is all one very long sentence—a prayer, actually. You might find reading this passage in a few different translations to be helpful. As you do your foundation work, begin looking for what Paul was praying for. Remember, our foundation work is time for us to slow down and get a grip of what is going on in this passage. If this is your first FOCUSed15 study, or you are super short on time today, hone in on verses 17–19. You can write out the verses word-for-word, diagram them, or draw pictures or symbols to help you begin to understand what is being said. There is no right or wrong way to do this. It is simply an exercise of intentionally taking in each word. We'll build on what we learn from this practice throughout the rest of the week.

3. Which words in Ephesians 1:15–21 impact you today?

4. Write out any questions you have about this passage. Your questions should be answered by the end of the week as you continue to study. If not, you'll have an opportunity to consult commentaries.

Ephesians, a letter written by the Apostle Paul to a mature church in the city of Ephesus, is filled with incredible truths about our new life in Christ. In fact, there is only one command given in three whole chapters: remember (Ephesians 2:11–12). Paul goes on to give many more exhortations in the second half of the letter, but he found it necessary to first write many words on God's glorious grace. Paul was passionate for God's people to fully understand where they came from and what they are called to; he was continually teaching doctrine, building up a lighthouse for the "brothers and sisters" he so deeply loved to look to.

We have hope, but we don't always understand or choose to remember the depth of what our hope is, which is why this prayer is a needed one. In the weeks to come, we will spend time studying more and more and more about the hope we have in Christ. Because we are forgetful people, and sometimes it takes 1,001 times of hearing something before we really, truly understand it. And if I fixate on my behavior, before I focus on my Liberator, I am bound to fall into the trap of hopeless legalism.

Jesus, I am so thankful for the hope You've given me! Holy Spirit, help me to understand better and better each day the hopeful riches I have in Christ. Create in me a spirit of remembrance, so that I may cling to the hope You have given me.

⁖ BONUS STUDY ⁖

1. Look up the background to Ephesians in a Bible dictionary or your study Bible, and fill out the fields below. (Remember, there are loads of free resources online. Check out KatieOrr.me/Resources for links.)

AUDIENCE: TO WHOM WAS THIS LETTER WRITTEN?	AIM: WHY WAS IT WRITTEN?

2. Read all of Ephesians. Consider making three lists:

WHAT IS TRUE OF ME BEFORE CHRIST?	WHAT IS TRUE OF ME AFTER CHRIST?	WHAT COMMANDS ARE GIVEN?

As you read through Ephesians, jot down anything that fits into one of these categories.

Observation

FOCUSing ON EPHESIANS 1:15–22

For it is you who light my lamp; the LORD my God lightens my darkness.

—PSALM 18:28

THE PHAROS LIGHTHOUSE, found in Alexandria, Egypt, towered for nearly 1,600 years before its final destruction by a series of earthquakes. This wonder of the ancient world was a pillar to the community and the seafarers looking for harbor. Pharos was built to be a navigation marker, a means of protection, as well as a status symbol of Alexander the Great, the leader behind the great city.

With the dawn of technological advances, lighthouses have lost much of their importance to today's mariners. But to the weary, uncertain sea-travellers of old, catching a glimpse of the Pharos Lighthouse would have been an instant source of relief, confidence, and assurance. Just as the ancient journeyman would be straining their eyes to see a glimmer of hope from that beacon of light, we too need to continually focus our eyes on the gospel. The hope of the gospel is our lighthouse. It is an ever-present guide meant to protect, to navigate, and to help us remember the great God who builds our hope.

Yesterday we began our trek through Paul's prayer to the church at Ephesus. Paul was an incredibly purposeful person, and I love that we have this prayer to model our own after.

1. Open your time with God through a prayer, expressing your eagerness to learn more about Him today. Ask the Holy Spirit to for His wisdom and revelation as we dive deeper into the truths held in these verses.

LOOK AT THE DETAILS

2. As you read Ephesians 1:15–21, look for what Paul requests of God. Take a deeper look at verses 16–18, and fill in the chart below.

WHAT PAUL DID	WHAT ACTIONS PAUL ASKED GOD TO TAKE

3. Now read the passage again, this time observing verses 18 and 19. We're getting closer to the main point, the anticipation of Paul's ceaseless praying. List out what he sees as the natural result of God's work. (If God gives them the Spirit of wisdom and revelation, and enlightens their hearts, what will result?)

4. Look back at your chart in Question 2. Why do you think Paul asked God to take these particular actions?

Wisdom. Revelation. Enlightenment.

Isn't that what we all need? In our deepest, darkest, hopeless days, for the light of the gospel to illuminate our hearts, just like it did at first. The hope of the gospel, our lighthouse is always there, shining on us. Yet—though we've been "saved" from sin—we sometimes live life in darkness. Though the promise of hope is somewhere in the back of our minds, it is not at the forefront of our moments. And, like a ship lost at sea, we need to find that ray of light to center us back on course.

But did you notice who brings the light? Enlightenment is a work of the Spirit, who is faithful to open our eyes to behold God's glory—even amidst the most difficult circumstances. So, if you are feeling hopeless today, like a ship lost at sea, and all you can see around you is darkness, lift up your head and ask the Spirit of God to enlighten your heart. He is always faithful to guide us.

> *Because of God's tender mercy, the morning light from heaven is about to break upon us, to give light to those who sit in darkness and in the shadow of death, and to guide us to the path of peace.*
>
> —LUKE 1:78–79 NLT

Jesus has come. He is our light, our beacon, our lighthouse. The Morning Light who always faithfully guides.

> *God, open my eyes! I want to see more and more and more of You every day. I want to experience the hope of the gospel in my every moment. Help me to hold fast to hope, as I better understand the depths of Your love for me and continually recall all that is true of me because of Christ. Thank You for Your grace.*

⁓ BONUS STUDY ⁓

Look up the following verses and note what you learn about God's illuminating presence.

2 Samuel 22:29	
Psalm 27:1	
Psalm 118:27	
Psalm 119:105	
Isaiah 60:1	
Luke 1:78–79	
1 Peter 2:9	

These verses only scratch the surface of the truth about God as our illuminator. For additional study, consider looking up the cross-references from these verses or use a Bible concordance to look up additional verses on light. Follow where the Spirit leads.

CHEAT SHEET

2. Read Ephesians 1:15–21 again looking for what Paul requests of God. Take a closer look at verses 16–18, and fill in the chart below.

WHAT PAUL DID	WHAT ACTIONS PAUL ASKED GOD TO TAKE
Did not cease to give thanks for them Remembered them	• Give them the Spirit of wisdom and revelation in the knowledge of Him • Enlighten their hearts

3. Now read the passage again, this time taking a closer look at verses 18 and 19. List out what Paul sees as the natural result of God's work. If God gives them the Spirit of wisdom and revelation, and enlightens their hearts, what will result?

That they would know:

• The hope to which they have been called

• The riches of their inheritance

• The immeasurable greatness of God's great power toward us who believe

Clarification

FOCUSing ON EPHESIANS 1:15–22

I LED MY first Bible study as a freshman at Auburn University. In the decades since, I've seen woman after woman go in and out of Bible study unchanged. They hear the words, maybe even verbally regurgitate truths, but their hearts remained unchanged. I've led some of those same studies, and remain unchanged. Experiencing the hope of the gospel is not about checking off our Bible study box. It is not an action we take, or an item we can buy to make things better. Nor can our hopelessness be changed by merely trying harder. The power of the gospel unfolds in our life as we allow the truths of God's Word to transform our minds.

We are all too prone to go through the motions and fail to let truth penetrate our hearts. I believe Paul saw this human tendency in his own ministry and in his own heart, thus his prayer expresses what we all truly need when we "lose" hope: to fully apprehend and desperately cling to the hope we have and the calling attached to it. To know of and appreciate the riches of all we've been given through Christ. To fathom and experience the immeasurable greatness of God's great power toward us.

Remember, hope is our lighthouse. It is meant to be a beacon in our lives to protect, to navigate, and to help us remember. All as we come to know—really know—the hope of the gospel in our lives.

1. Open today's time with prayer, thanking God for the depths of His living and active Word. Ask Him to make you aware of the places you are not allowing God's Word to penetrate your heart. Ask His Spirit to grant a willingness

to change, and the grace to follow in obedience to where He is leading.

UNCOVER THE ORIGINAL MEANING

Today we come to clarification day, our Greek study. You may be a bit intimidated by the thought of studying the original language, but it's an important layer we get to peel back. Studying the Greek can be as simple as looking up a word in the dictionary with the right tools. If this is your first attempt at Greek study, I encourage you to check out the videos I've created to show you how to use many of the online Greek tools. Just head to KatieOrr.me/Resources and look for the videos section.

Step 1: DECIDE which English word you would like to study.

To start your Greek study, look for any potential key words in Ephesians 1:15–21. As you find any repeated word or words that seem important to the passage, write them down below.

Maybe you had the word *hope* in your list? Let's study this word together.

Step 2: DISCOVER the Greek word in an interlinear Bible.

Now that you know what you want to study, you can look up the English word *hope* in an interlinear Bible to find out what the original Greek word is. An interlinear Bible will show you English verses and line up each word next to the Greek words they were translated from.

Let's take the phrase in Ephesians 1:18 that contains our word *hope*, to see how this works: "that you may know what is the *hope* to which he has called you."

In Greek, it looks like this: "εἰς τὸ εἰδέναι ὑμᾶς τίς ἐστιν ἡ ἐλπὶς τῆς κλήσεως" (GNT Morph).

Most people (including me!) can't read this, so the transliteration of the Greek is often provided for us as well. This transliteration is the Greek turned into words that use English letters to spell out how the Greek is read. For example, the first Greek words we see, "εἰς" and "τὸ," are transliterated into "eis" and "ho," which is how they are pronounced.

The interlinear Bible simply lines up the two versions (and usually the transliteration as well) so we can see which word goes with which, like this:

εἰς τὸ	εἰδέναι	ὑμᾶς	τίς'	ἐστιν ἡ	ἐλπὶς	τῆς	κλήσεως
eis ho	oida	sy	tis	eimi ho	elpis	ho	klesis
so that	will know	you	what	is	hope	the	calling

Now you can use this layout to find the original word for *hope*. Do you see it?

hope = elpis = ἐλπὶς

Step 3: DEFINE that Greek word using a Greek lexicon.

Now that you know the original word for *hope* used in Ephesians 1:18 is *elpis*, you can look up that Greek word in a Greek lexicon (which is like a dictionary) and note the following:

Lexicon discovery: elpis

• Definition: hope, expectation

- Times used: 54

- Part of speech: noun

- Other ways it is translated: hope, faith, hopes

- Any special notes: Strong's Greek #1680; "From a primary elpō (to antici-
  pate, usually with pleasure)"

Pretty simple, right?

Now, why don't you try it on your own? Use the steps above to look up the word *riches* in verse 18. Don't forget the list of free resources at KatieOrr.me/Resources, including videos explaining how to find and use an interlinear Bible and Greek lexicon. (If you are not ready to try studying the Greek, skip all this and just look up the word in the dictionary, then simply write out the definition.)

riches =

Lexicon discovery:

- Definition:

- Times used:

- Part of speech:

- Other ways it is translated:

- Any special notes:

2. What discoveries did you make through your clarification study?

As I look back on my own seasons of hopelessness, I notice a pattern, one that mimics the cry of Paul's heart for his people. My hopelessness stems from either not understanding the gospel or not remembering the gospel.

Early on in my walk with God (my crawling, toddling days) my mind was filled with so many different voices, many of which were not preaching the true gospel. I was hearing "do this" and "don't do that"—all good things meant to keep me out of trouble, but instead led me to be gospel-confused. I thought the gospel was "do these things and don't do those things, and God will love you." So when I found my heart lacking a desire for the good yet a strong craving for the bad, it left me horribly baffled. Maybe I wasn't really saved at all? So, I would secretly rededicate my life, or walk down the aisle yet again, assuming I must have missed a part of the equation the last time around. Until I began to hear the real gospel. The gospel of grace, the truth that it is not about what I've done or what I will do, but it is all about what Jesus did on my behalf.

If the gospel is fuzzy to you like it was to me, I encourage you to keep learning. Keep searching Scripture. We cannot hold on to something we don't understand. And the Bible is very clear that we receive the gospel by grace through faith. If you are experiencing day after day after day of hopelessness, it may be that you don't understand the gospel at all. If you feel this is the case, you may need to put this study down and go back to the basics. (You can read more about the gospel in the appendix.) Seek out a trusted mentor, pastor, or friend, and ask them to explain the bare bones gospel to you.

Even if we understand the basics of the gospel, we are a forgetful people, which is why we need to hear the truth of the gospel over and over again. Just this week, because of my forgetfulness, I experienced hopelessness. It is so easy to forget the gospel-truths about myself. That I am already accepted, loved, chosen, and forgiven. I don't need to spin my wheels to win God's approval. I already have it. And it wasn't until I began to cling to these truths and remember that God is for me, not against me that I began to experience the peace and hope in my places of hopelessness.

Just like a lighthouse that continues to shine in the storm, twirling its bright line of hope for the weary one, we need to see the hope of the gospel before us again and again. 'Round and 'round shining and proclaiming, "I'm here . . . I'm here . . . I'm here . . . Keep your eyes on Me. I know the waves are crashing on you and you can't quite see in front of you as far as you would like. But I'm your beacon. Your hope for change, and for all good things to come. You are not forgotten. You are not lost. You are not without hope."

When I cannot see hope, it's not because hope is not there. The hope of the gospel is all around me—ever present—through His glory beheld in the sunset to the presence of His Spirit in my soul. If I am in Christ, I always have hope. Regardless of my circumstances. So, if I cannot see hope, it's not because hope has moved, it's because I am forgetful.

Hopelessness = forgetfulness.

God, make me to continually remember all You've done for me! Tune my heart to sing of Your grace. Bring people in my life who will shine the gospel truth to me again and again and again. Holy Spirit, give me Your discernment to know if the teachings I am listening to are gospel-centered or works-centered. Thank You for the hope I have because of all Christ has done for me.

⋅!⋅ BONUS STUDY ⋅!⋅

Follow the previous steps for as many words as you have time for. Feel free to simply look up the definition for the Greek word, especially if this is your first try. There is much to be learned even in that!

Here are a few words you could look up, but feel free to look up any word that catches your eye.

ENLIGHTENED (v. 18)	IMMEASURABLE (v. 19)	KNOW (v. 18)

CHEAT SHEET

Step 3: DEFINE that Greek word using a Greek lexicon.

Now that you know the original word for "hope" used in Ephesians 1:18 is elpis, you can look up that Greek word in a Greek lexicon (which is like a dictionary).

riches = ploutos

Lexicon discovery: ploutos

• Definition: riches, wealth

• Times used: 22

• Part of speech: noun

• Other ways it is translated: wealth

• Any special notes: Strong's Greek #4149; Also used in Ephesians 1:7, 2:7 "riches of his grace," Ephesians 3:16, "riches of glory" grants us strength with power through the Holy Spirit. God will supply every need according to his "riches in glory in Christ Jesus" (Philippians 4:19).

Utilization

FOCUSing ON EPHESIANS 1:15–22

Send out your light and your truth; let them lead me; let them bring me to your holy hill and to your dwelling!

—Psalm 43:3

OUR MOVE TO Kentucky put me the furthest away from the equator I've ever lived. I knew winters would be colder, and in preparation, I mentally readied myself for the long, cold, icy days. However, there is one aspect of Kentucky winters I wasn't prepared for: the lack of sunshine. Week after week the days are gray and gloomy, on top of being frigid. Not only is the cloud cover apparent, but there is a dramatic difference in the hours of sunlight. It remains just a bit darker every morning and the sun sets earlier each evening. This makes for an even colder, gloomier winter season. Reminding myself that it will get warmer and I will see the sun again goes a long way to enduring those long, dark, frigid days.

One thing is true: the sun always shines, even when it's negative two degrees and pitch black. However, my experience of the sun is much different in the dead of February than in the heat of July. Our lives, too, are seasonal, and just because we can't always see and feel the warmth of God's presence, doesn't mean He is not with us. Our lighthouse of hope always shines. The truth of the gospel is always present. Sometimes we just need a reminder—an enlightening—to help us remember what we already possess.

This is what Paul prays for his dear church members (and applies to you and me): illumination—a work of God to open the eyes of our hearts—so that we would know, really know, three things:

- The hope to which we have been called
- The riches of our inheritance
- The immeasurable greatness of God's great power toward us

To deeply understanding and experience these truths is a work of God. One that we are desperately dependent on the Holy Spirit to open our eyes to.

1. Spend some time today praying for these three things to be true in your life. Ask God to show you what keeps you from truly knowing that you are called, that you are rich in Christ, and that God is great in power.

DISCOVER THE CONNECTIONS

2. Read Ephesians 1:15–21 to start your study today.

3. For our utilization study, we simply look up verses related to any word or phrase we want to learn more about. Today, we'll start with the phrase "the hope to which He has called you" in verse 18. Look up each reference in the following chart and take notes from any passages that reveal a bigger picture of the threads this verse is attached to. You might consider applying one or more of the FOCUS method steps to that passage, depending on the time you have to spend for the day. I typically enjoy listing out truths I see,

especially those that help me understand the original passage I'm studying. You can write out the passage in the space provided, or even look up a word or two in your interlinear Bible. Just do what interests you and what you have time for!

1:18—"THE HOPE TO WHICH HE HAS CALLED YOU"				
Ephesians 4:1–4	Hebrews 3:1	Philippians 3:14	1 Peter 5:10	Romans 8:28

God's illuminating work affords the opportunity to know the hope of the Gospel better and better every day, regardless of our circumstances. Our part is to appropriately respond to God's grace in our lives—even when we can't see it. Continually remember all He has already done. We once were lost, but now are found. We were dead, without hope, orphaned, and alone. But God rescued us from our helpless state and gave us new life with a new, heavenly calling—a life to be lived with our eyes wide open.

Yet, all too often I let the waves of my ever-changing emotions drive me. Instead, I must determine to look ahead for the ray of hope that is always there.

> *Though I feel aimless, I can know I have been called with great purpose.*

> *Though I feel like a beggar, I can know I am rich in Christ.*

> *Though I feel helpless, I can know I have the power of Christ within me.*

> *Though I feel lost, I can know I can have been found and rescued from the power of sin and death.*

> *Though I feel defeated, I can know that through Christ, I am victorious.*

The list goes on and on. Hope is a gift, something you and I could never provide for ourselves, yet our experience of God's gift of hope depends on how well we depend on it. And so, to hold on to hope, we must fight to understand and remember the gospel and the calling we've been given because of it. There is a great purpose we have been given, and our days are to be filled with the hope-filled calling of the gospel.

> *God, grant me a fresh vision for Your calling on my life. Help me to see my days in light of eternity, and give me the grace to walk forward in confidence in Your specific plan for me.*

⋅!⋅ BONUS STUDY ⋅!⋅

Look up cross-references for additional phrases in this week's passage that you would like to learn more about. Continue until you need to move on with your day. If your Bible does not have cross-references in it, check out the online cross-referencing recommendations at KatieOrr .me/Resources.

You could easily spend two or three days, 15 minutes or more at a time, working through each verse. Remember, these days are simply suggestions. Follow God's leading. If He tells you to slow down and dig deep, go for it!

CHEAT SHEET

3. For our utilization study, we simply look up verses related to any word or phrase we want to learn more about. Today, we'll start with the phrase "the hope to which he has called you" in verse 18.

1:18—"THE HOPE TO WHICH HE HAS CALLED YOU"				
Ephesians 4:1–4	Hebrews 3:1	Philippians 3:14	1 Peter 5:10	Romans 8:28
There is a certain manner I can walk that is worthy of my calling: • Humility • Gentleness • Patience • Bearing with one another in love • Eager to maintain the unity of the Spirit, in the bond of peace • I am called to one hope/one calling	I share in a heavenly calling.	I have an upward/heavenly call This call is of God, in Christ This call has an end goal, with a prize attached to it	Called to God's eternal glory in Christ	Called according to God's purpose God works all things together for good, according to that purpose/calling

My high calling = the hope I've been given = my upward call = the prize to press on toward

Summation

FOCUSing ON EPHESIANS 1:15–22

Don't copy the behavior and customs of this world, but let
God transform you into a new person by changing the way
you think. Then you will learn to know God's will for you,
which is good and pleasing and perfect.

—ROMANS 12:2 NLT

I GREW UP in the High Desert, a section of the Mojave Desert that California locals call "up the hill." From the Los Angeles basin, you literally have to go up into the mountains, along the San Andreas Fault, where you find yourself on the other side in an arid desert climate at an elevation of 2,800 feet above sea level. Though we didn't get much rain there, when it did shower, the water had plenty of thirsty land, dry creek beds, and lakes to dump into. As I recall, flooding in the High Desert was never an issue.

Living in "the South," we experience flooding all the time. Rainfall is much more plentiful and consistent. There is a very small creek that runs past our house in rural Kentucky. When it rains, that tiny, harmless creek turns into a raging threat to the road and houses around it. Since the ground is already saturated, the new rainfall cannot penetrate the soil, and what is meant for life and nourishment becomes a nuisance and a potential for danger.

God's Word is never a nuisance, but is important to remember that quantity is not necessarily better than quality. A lifetime of abundant yet shallow Bible reading will not bring forth the same fruit as a careful, deep study of the Bible. Interestingly, I see a greater thirst for truth in the spiritually "dry" places, compared to the saturated places where there's a church on every corner. We must be careful not to equate being surrounded by God's Word with allowing our hearts to be penetrated with God's Word. This is why our summation day is crucial to transformation. It's easy to run from church service to Bible study to an inspirational Pinterest quote, but never let the truth contained within each to penetrate our souls. We can be saturated with truth yet drowning in hopelessness.

We're all in need of the presence of God's Word in our hearts. Today, let's slow down and take some time to allow all we've learned to seep deep down into the soil of our lives, and not allow it to drift away without changing us.

RESPOND TO GOD'S WORD

Today, let's take some time to slow down and digest what we've been learning by going through our summation steps. Remember, this is when we begin to answer the question, "How should what I've learned affect me?" To do this we will do three things:

IDENTIFY — Find the main idea of each passage.

MODIFY — Evaluate my beliefs in light of the main idea.

GLORIFY — Align my life to reflect the truth of God's Word.

1. Imagine your heart as a dry and dusty land, in desperate need of rain. Ask God to come and fill the gaps and cracks with the truths of His Word, bringing a fullness only His presence can provide.

IDENTIFY: What's the main idea?

Take a few moments to flip back to each day's study to review what you've learned.

2. Write out Ephesians 1:15–21 in your own words. Or simply write out what you think the main idea of Ephesians 1:15–21 is in regard to our study of hope.

3. Read a commentary or study Bible to see how your observations from this week line up with the scholars. As you search the commentaries, ask God to make clear the meaning of any passages that are fuzzy to you. Record any additional observations below.

MODIFY: How do my beliefs line up to this main idea?

4. How does my view of hopelessness line up with what I've learned this week?

5. What is one area I am currently experiencing hopelessness? Which of the two causes of hopelessness am I most likely experiencing? (Am I gospel-confused, or gospel-forgetful?)

6. How can knowing the calling of my hope, the riches of my inheritance, and the immeasurable greatness of God's power help me hold on to hope?

GLORIFY: In light of this main idea, how can I realign my life to best reflect God's glory?

7. What adjustments can I make to allow these truths to penetrate my soul?

8. Pick one adjustment and write it down below. Ask God for the grace to walk obediently this week, as you battle hopelessness with the truth of the gospel.

Holding on to hope is a battle. A continual striving to understand and remember the gospel. If you are experiencing hopelessness, know that you are not alone. Not only that, but I pray after this week's study you can see a way out during your dark days. The root cause of most hopelessness is simple forgetfulness. Know that I am fighting this battle of forgetfulness right alongside of you. I am praying for us to remember and know deep down that we are loved, forgiven, and precious to God.

If we are in Christ, we cannot lose hope. If we have placed our faith in Christ alone we have Christ, "the hope of glory," within us (Colossians 1:27).

I need You, God. I have no hope for change without Your grace. Be my strength. Open my eyes. Change my heart. Be glorified in me!

.⸱'⸱. BONUS STUDY .⸱'⸱.

Consider writing out Ephesians 1:15–21 or another verse God has put on your heart onto a few 3x5 cards. Keep the verses with you, post them up around your house, and commit them to memory. Cling to truth as you move forward.

FOCUSING ON **HEBREWS 6:17–20**

Hope Is My Anchor

❦

Foundation

FOCUSing ON HEBREWS 6:17–20

SOME OF MY earliest and most cherished memories are from the lake. Summer after summer, I was pulled into a bright orange lifejacket and enjoyed the speed of a ski boat. I still enjoy the thrilling yet calming wind against my face in daddy's boat. We spent many summer weekends together with my grandparents, uncles, and family friends at various lakes across California. One summer my grandparents rented a houseboat for the week, and we enjoyed a restful, fun-filled week of family time and waterskiing.

Cruising along the water can be a calming way to spend a day. It can also be a nightmare if you're not prepared. If you own a boat, you also own lifejackets, a paddle, and an anchor. Without an anchor, the boat is subject to the whims of the weather and the waves it brings. Whether your vessel is big or small, an anchor is a necessity.

An anchor serves as a way to connect the boat to an immovable source of security. When we lived on that houseboat, we were sure to put the anchor down once we found a good spot to rest. If we all went to bed without the anchor secured, who knows where the boat would have drifted while we slept. We might have found ourselves lost in the middle of the lake, or run aground with a rock-sized hole in the hull.

Every boat needs an anchor. Every believer in Christ is given an anchor—a strong and steadfast gospel-hope in good things to come. But just like every ship's captain has a choice to use this safeguard, we must also be sure our anchor is down and rooted into the foundation of our faith in Jesus. This week's passage will have much to show us about the anchor we have and its importance in our experience of hope as we choose to hold fast to the mooring given us in Christ.

Spend a few moments to reflect on your life right now. Close your eyes and imagine yourself in a boat in the middle of the sea. Envision the movement of the waves around you. Are they big? Small? Calm? Oppressive? Now look down on yourself? Are you seasick and dizzy, still trying to find your "sea legs"? Or are you peaceful and sure, regardless of the waves surrounding you?

1. Circle the words that best describe your experience in life's boat over the past few months.

Steadfast	Unpredictable	Dark	Lost	Wavering
Cold	Secure	Oppressive	Dizzying	Smooth
	Confident	Steady	Calm	

2. Write down any other words that come to mind:

ENJOY EVERY WORD

3. Today we'll work through our first layer of studying Hebrews 6:17–20 by writing the passage in whichever way you enjoy. Do something to help you

slow down and enjoy what is communicated in these verses.
Remember, there is no right or wrong way to do this. It is simply an exercise of intentionally taking in each word. We'll build on what we learn from this practice throughout the rest of the week.

4. We're starting to see the main point of the passage. What do you think it might be? What do you think these verses communicate? It's OK if you are not entirely sure. We still have many layers to peel back and make discoveries that will help us better understand the meaning.

The storms of life can leave us tattered and torn. And though we each have an anchor—our gospel hope in Christ—we may not always be using that anchor correctly. I'm praying God's Spirit would continue the work of illumination this week, so we can each see where our hope is really placed.

> God, help me to see where I've let down my anchor. Do I have it deeply rooted into Your character or is it waving around the middle of the sea? Show me how to let my anchor sink deep down into the truth of who You are and all the promises You have for me. Help me to hold fast to that anchor when I feel tattered and torn. By Your grace alone, I will cling.

⁃!⁃ BONUS STUDY ⁃!⁃

Take some time to read through the Book of Hebrews. Pay special attention to all that is being taught about Christ. Consider making a list of all the names, titles, and descriptive words given for Jesus.

NAMES	TITLES	DESCRIPTIVE WORDS

Observation

FOCUSing ON HEBREWS 6:17–20

I have said these things to you, that in me you may have peace. In the world you will have tribulation. But take heart; I have overcome the world.

—JOHN 16:33

I GET ALL fired up when I hear "preachers" saying God wants me to be happy, healthy, and wealthy. "You deserve more, better," they say. "Just set your mind to something and go for it. God is for you. He will give you what you desire if you love and obey Him enough. Have faith, and life will go well for you."

Problem is, these are half-truths—shadows of Scripture. Sound bites that are close enough to sound right and are highly motivational, but in actuality, hold devastating implications. When life doesn't go our way we wonder what we did wrong or what we didn't do enough of to get God to act on our behalf. And when life is peachy-keen, our need for God dissipates. We turn Christianity into a formula to be figured out and followed.

Fact is, we are not promised smooth sailing. We are not guaranteed to bypass the difficult storms of life just because we are Christians. And the presence of a squall does not mean God is upset with us. I've found the opposite to be true in my life. The trials I've faced have proved God to be lovingly present, tenderly purposeful, and powerfully able to use all things for my good. I've learned that being a Christian doesn't give me some force-field bubble that protects me from harm. But having the hope of Christ within me—knowing and holding onto all He has done for me and all that He will do—brings a deep-down peace that no positive-thinking prosperity message can provide.

I'll say it again: walking with God is not a formula to be found out and followed. Abundant life with Jesus is a journey of continually drawing near to His presence while holding fast to the gospel—our anchor of truth. Remember, all who are in Christ possess the treasure of hope? It's a noun, not a verb. But we've learned we don't always experience the hope-filled abundant life because we either don't truly know the gospel or we forget.

Consider these three pictures:

UNANCHORED

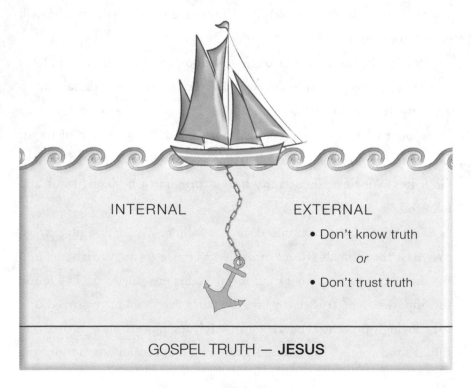

INTERNAL

EXTERNAL

• Don't know truth

or

• Don't trust truth

GOSPEL TRUTH — **JESUS**

ANCHORED YET DANGLING

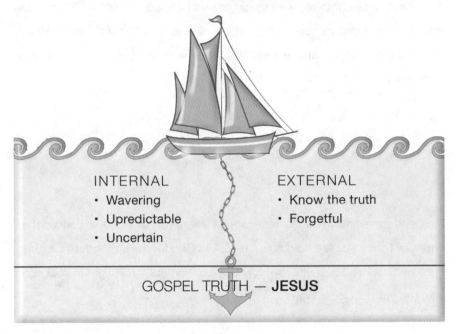

INTERNAL
- Wavering
- Upredictable
- Uncertain

EXTERNAL
- Know the truth
- Forgetful

GOSPEL TRUTH – **JESUS**

ANCHORED AND CLINGING

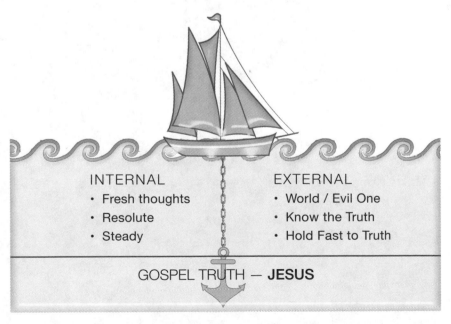

INTERNAL
- Fresh thoughts
- Resolute
- Steady

EXTERNAL
- World / Evil One
- Know the Truth
- Hold Fast to Truth

GOSPEL TRUTH – **JESUS**

1. Compare these images with the words you circled yesterday. Think of the last storm you experienced. Envision yourself as you ride the waves. Which of the three voyages above best describes your experience through your difficulties?

2. Spend some time in honest reflection of where you've let down your anchor, and how tightly you are holding on to it. Ask God for the strength to be forthright with your reality. Invite the Holy Spirit to continue to enlighten your days with the truth of God's Word.

LOOK AT THE DETAILS

We often want to measure growth with external charts and checkboxes, but I believe true spiritual growth cannot be evaluated simply by our deeds. Actions can be modified. Attitudes can be mimicked. But holding fast to hope cannot be faked. As we move on to our observation day, I pray your eyes would continually be opened to see more of who God is.

If our view of God is big, the reality of our hope will be big, too.

3. Read Hebrews 6:17–20, looking first for truths about God. Record your findings in the chart below. Then read the passage again and look for the actions God took. These two sentences are brimming full of truths. Don't try to figure out what it all means, just write what you see.

TRUTHS ABOUT GOD	ACTIONS OF GOD

If you are unfamiliar with the inner place, curtain of the holy of holies, and the position of high priest, I encourage you to take a few moments today to look over Understanding the Ceremonial Law in the appendix to understand its importance.

4. Take one more look at Hebrews 6:17–20, this time looking for what is true about the gospel hope we have in Jesus.

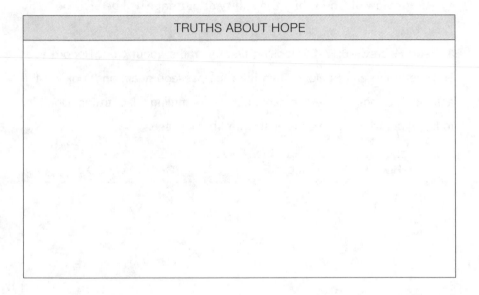

TRUTHS ABOUT HOPE

5. Which of the truths you studied today stands out to you?

God, I confess the places where I have not trusted in Your promises. Help me to see that You are steadfast and sure. Open my eyes to see You more and more each day.

⁃!⁃ BONUS STUDY ⁃!⁃

Using a Bible dictionary, look up any terms or names you are unfamiliar with or would like to learn more about. Write down what you learn. The following are a few suggestions.

THE INNER PLACE	THE CURTAIN	THE HIGH PRIEST	MELCHIZEDEK

CHEAT SHEET

3. Read Hebrews 6:17–20, looking first for truths about God. Record your findings in the chart below. Then read the passage again and look for the actions God took.

TRUTHS ABOUT GOD	ACTIONS OF GOD
• He desires to help me understand Him (v. 17) • Unchangeable character (v. 17) • Unchangeable purpose (v. 17) • The promise and the oath are unchangeable (vv. 17, 18) • It is impossible for God to lie (v. 18) • Jesus has gone into the inner place, behind the curtain (v. 20) • Jesus is the forerunner on our behalf (v. 20) • Jesus is the high priest, forever after the order of Melchizedek (v. 20)	• Desired to convince the "heirs of promise" of His faithful character • He guaranteed His promise with an oath

4. Take one more look at Hebrews 6:17–20, this time looking for what is true about the gospel hope we have in Jesus.

TRUTHS ABOUT HOPE
I can have strong encouragement to hold fast to hope
Hope is set before me
Sure and steadfast anchor of the soul
Enters into the inner place, behind the curtain with Jesus

Clarification

FOCUSing ON HEBREWS 6:17–20

WHEN MY HUSBAND Chris and I sold our first home, we had a bit of a scuffle with the buyers. The kitchen in our townhouse was fairly large, though it lacked sufficient counter space. When we first moved into it, we purchased a pricey island to fill the expanse as well as provide extra storage and room to cook. We loved this island. However, the kitchen in our next house had plenty of counter room and not enough floor space for the large island. We hated to let it go, but felt we didn't have the time or energy to try to sell it amidst the chaos of packing and moving. So we put off dealing with it. As we got closer to the closing date, the buyers asked us (through our agents) what we intended to do with the island, and we flippantly mentioned we would leave it.

A few days later, Chris's grandparents asked to purchase it from us. A perfect solution! We don't have to worry about trying to coordinate a sale, yet still get some cash from it. As you can imagine, the buyers were not happy with this, and left no room for doubt about their disgust with our change of mind. Though we unwisely promised something without checking our options thoroughly, and we felt badly about shifting our decision, there was nothing in writing about the island. The island was our property and there was no legal bind in place to make us keep our word about leaving it behind.

This week's passage teaches that we have a double guarantee, by two unchangeable things: a promise and an oath. Like our buyers, you might find yourself disappointed in a promise from men because people's minds and circumstances change. But this is not the case with God. He is steadfast and unchangeable. If He promises us an island, we will get the island. A promise from God is enough, but He didn't stop there. Maybe because He knows how fickle and shortsighted we are, He confirmed His promise with an oath—a binding and unbreakable contract. He did this because He desired to show us more convincingly that He can be trusted. His promises are sure. We are safe to hold fast to the hope we have in the gospel. The unchangeable, glorious, life-giving gospel.

1. Take a look at your view of God's promises. Do you see them as final, or do you wonder if He is going to change His mind about you? Ask Him to open your heart to receive His promises and to strengthen your faith to trust in His oath.

UNCOVER THE ORIGINAL MEANING

Here we go again! I know that this day can seem daunting and difficult if this is a new skill. When we first learn to ride a bike or figure out the latest technology, it can be frustrating, but the rewards of pressing in and continuing on are worth it!

If the thought of studying the Greek is still too much, consider selecting a few words to look up in the dictionary, then write the verse with the definitions in place of the words you looked up. Remember, no Bible study method is perfect. Do what works for you.

Step 1: DECIDE which English word you would like to study.

To start your Greek study, look for any potential keywords in Hebrews 6:17–20. As you find any repeated word or words that seem important to the passage, write them down below.

Step 2: DISCOVER the Greek word in an interlinear Bible.

There are so many great words to look up, but I want to make sure you look up at least one today: *unchangeable*. (Your version might use immutable.) Using an interlinear Bible, find the original word for "unchangeable" used in verses 17 and 18 and write it below.

Immutable =

Step 3: DEFINE that Greek word using a Greek lexicon.

Now we can look up the Greek word in a Greek lexicon (which is like a dictionary) and note the following:

Lexicon discovery: ametathetos

• Definition: unalterable, immutable

• Times used: 2

• Part of speech: adjective

• Other ways it is translated: immutable

• Any special notes: Strongs #276; used only here in this passage;
  "unchanging, unchangeable, never to change"

Follow the above steps to look up one more word. Here are a few words to choose from:

Desired (v. 17)

Guaranteed (v. 17)

Hold fast (v. 18)

Lexicon discovery:

• Definition:

• Times used:

• Part of speech:

• Other ways it is translated:

• Any special notes:

2. What discoveries did you make through your clarification study? Which word did you learn the most about?

God desired. God guaranteed. Our unalterable God wanted to give us double assurance that our hope in Him and all He provides is indeed a sure and steadfast hope. Do you see His grace in every move here? A promise from the One who spoke the heavens into place should be enough, but He knows the reality of our wavering, distrusting hearts, and instead of being disgusted and disappointed by our inability to believe, He covers our failures with the comforting blanket of His love and moves even closer. He puts an oath on top of the promise, not because He felt He needed to prove Himself to us, but because He desired—He willed—to do whatever it takes for us to understand His love for us. In so doing, He guaranteed—He pledged—the promise with a double assurance of His character.

At the foundation of our hope, our faith, our everything, is the character of God. If we have His character mixed up in our head, we have everything mixed up. We must strive to know and hold fast to the steadfast character of God. Without Him, and a clear and growing view of who He is, we are truly without hope.

> *God, forgive me for making my walk with You about things and actions and events. Help me to pour all my devotion into knowing You better. Don't allow me to continue to be busy with activities that do not point me to my great need for my great God. Show me how to know You better each day. Continue to draw me closer and closer to You. Take off the blinders that keep me from seeing You as You really are. Reveal to me the lies that I believe about who You are or who You are not. I am desperate for You.*

⁻⸬⁻ BONUS STUDY ⁻⸬⁻

Look up additional words in Hebrews 6:17–20 to discover their original meaning.

CHEAT SHEET

Step 3: DEFINE that Greek word using a Greek lexicon.

Desired = boulomai

Lexicon discovery: boulomai

• Definition: wish, will, be willing, purpose

• Times used: 38

• Part of speech: verb

• Other ways it is translated: will, would, be minded, intend, be disposed,
  be willing

• Any special notes: Strongs #1014

Guaranteed = mesiteuō

Lexicon discovery: mesiteuō

• Definition: guarantee

• Times used: 1

• Part of speech: verb

• Other ways it is translated: interpose, intervene, convey

• Any special notes: Strongs #3315; "cause agreement, bring about a mutually
  accepted agreement between to parties; confirm;" from root word mesitēs,
  which translates to mediator, or reconciler; "to pledge one's self, give surety."

Hold fast = krateō

Lexicon discovery: krateō

• Definition: be strong, take possession of

• Times used: 47

• Part of speech: verb

• Other ways it is translated: hold, take, lay hold on, take by, lay hold upon,
  lay hand on

• Any special notes: Strongs #2902; "to hold fast, i.e. not discard or let go.
  to keep carefully and faithfully."

Utilization

FOCUSing ON HEBREWS 6:17–20

THOUGH I SPENT my summers on the lake, I'm not the best water skier. I must have had one too many wipeouts early on because there are too many factors that scare me. Going outside of the wake of the boat is a rarity, and if the slack on the rope is not something I can reel in quick enough, I bail. You see, if there is slack on the rope, the ride is jerky. When the ride is jerky, I feel out of control. And when I feel out of control, I'm done. Skiing is then no longer a fun event. Instead, it's a scary ride.

1. Take a look again at our boat drawings. What do you notice about the chain in the "anchored yet wavering" middle picture?

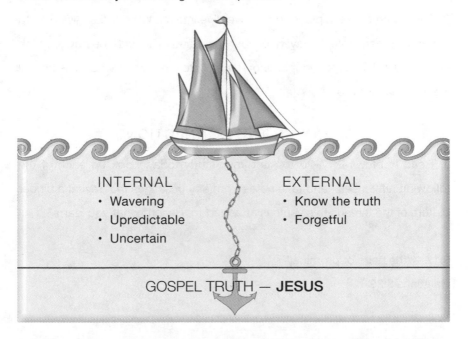

INTERNAL
• Wavering
• Upredictable
• Uncertain

EXTERNAL
• Know the truth
• Forgetful

GOSPEL TRUTH — **JESUS**

There is quite a bit of slack, isn't there? Compare that to the "anchored and clinging" image on the right. It's a monumental difference to ride in a boat ride with lots of slack versus floating in a boat tightly held to the anchor below. If there is too much slack, and a wave strikes, there is more room for the vessel to spin out of control. The journey is much more unpredictable and uncertain. However, if the chain is tightly bound, the ride will be steady. It doesn't make the waves any smaller or the rain any warmer, but the experience of the troublesome storms are much more endurable.

Here is where faith comes into play with our experience of hope. If you've gone through my *Everyday Faith* Bible study, you know that faith is drawing near to the presence of God. By faith, we draw our ship nearer to the anchor—our hope in the gospel—and hold fast. Hope-filled living comes when we actively and intentionally keep a tight connection to God and the truth of the gospel.

2. Spend some time in prayer before we dive into the Word today. Ask God to continue to penetrate the layers of your heart and mind with the power of the gospel. Ask Him to root your anchor deeply into the truth of who He is and all He has done for you.

DISCOVER THE CONNECTIONS

3. Read Hebrews 6:17–20 to start your study today. Look up each of the following references, and take notes from any passages that reveal a bigger picture of the threads this verse is attached to. Record what you learn.

6:17 — "the heirs of promise"
Galatians 3:29

6:18—"it is impossible for God to lie"

Titus 1:2

6:20—"as a forerunner on our behalf"

Hebrews 4:14

Hebrews 9:24

God doesn't want us to hope better. He desires for us to hold fast to hope. God gifted us hope through Christ and it is already firmly and forever attached to our boat. However, the abundant life we are promised is experienced best when we let our hope-anchor sink securely into the foundation of God's love for us. And once it is deeply rooted in truth, our job is to hold fast to the truth with all we are. Truth is our tether, and it will help us to see God in our every moment—both the calm and the crazy.

> *Thank You for the gift of hope. Thank You Jesus, for dying for my sins so that I can enter into a relationship with You. I am truly in awe of Your love for me. Humbled by Your sacrifice. Thankful for all I can hope for, because of all You've done for me. Be glorified in me today.*

⁙ BONUS STUDY ⁙

Look up any additional cross-references in Hebrews 6:17–20 that you would like to learn more about.

CHEAT SHEET

3. Read Hebrews 6:17–20 to start your study today. Look up each reference below and take notes from any passages that reveal a bigger picture of the threads this verse is attached to. Record what you learn below.

6:17 — "the heirs of promise"

Galatians 3:29 — all who are in Christ = Abraham's offspring = heirs of promise

6:18 — "it is impossible for God to lie"

Titus 1:2 — God, who never lies, promised us the hope of eternal life, even before the world began.

6:20 — "as a forerunner on our behalf"

Hebrews 4:14 — since Jesus is our forerunner and high priest, we should hold fast to our confession of faith

Hebrews 9:24 — Jesus not only entered the holy place here on earth, but entered into the holy place of heaven, where He appears to God on our behalf

Summation

FOCUSing ON HEBREWS 6:17-20

My soul clings to you; your right hand upholds me.

—Psalm 63:8

DO YOU RECALL what it was like to swing as a child? Remember the thrill of the wind in your face and the butterflies in your stomach during that brief second when your direction changes from upward to downward? There is a happiness, calm, and excitement every child enjoys once they learn to embrace the fun of the swing. Oftentimes, kids can be fairly timid about the swing at first. When my little ones learned to swing, I covered their tiny, chubby hands with my own because it took them a while to understand the importance of keeping a tight hold on the swing's chains. This way, when they let go or simply forgot to keep holding on, they didn't fall because my hands surrounded theirs. I held on for them.

There are many commands in the Bible, but really so many of them all boil down to the same: Abide. Remain. Hold Fast. Keep in step. Draw near. Stay on guard. The Christian life is all about holding on and staying connected to the source of all we need—the gospel of Christ.

I long to be "anchored and clinging"—for a lifetime. Not just today, tomorrow, or next week, but to the end. But if I'm honest, the thought of holding fast for a lifetime is wearying. I cannot hold fast forever, on my own. It takes a lot of hard work, yes. But it also takes a whole lot of grace. Without the sustaining power of God's glorious grace in my life, I cannot endure to the end. I cannot hold on—I will not hold on—without His hands surrounding mine.

Staying "anchored and clinging" is all about grace. By His grace we were given the anchor of hope. By His grace we are forever and securely chained to the gospel. By His grace we hold fast to this chain, pulling it ever closer each day. So, let's cling to grace, knowing that grace is clinging to us. Grace is God's big, strong, capable hands that gently—yet firmly—cover my weak, trembling, weary fingers.

RESPOND TO GOD'S WORD

IDENTIFY: What's the main idea?

Take a few moments to flip back to each days' studies and review what you've learned.

1. Write out Hebrews 6:17–20 in your own words. Or simply write out what you think the main idea of Hebrews 6:17–20 is in regard to our study of hope.

2. Read a commentary or study Bible to see how your observations line up. As you search the commentaries, ask God to make clear the meaning of any passages that are fuzzy to you. Record any additional observations.

If you still have any lingering questions about this week's verse, ask a trusted pastor, mentor, or friend what they think about the verse or enter the online discussion at BibleStudyHub.com.

MODIFY: How do my beliefs line up to this main idea?

3. How does your experience of hope line up with what you've learned this week?

4. How does your view of God line up with what you've learned this week?

5. How could holding fast to hope—anchored and clinging—affect your everyday moments?

GLORIFY: In light of this main idea, how can I realign my life to best reflect God's glory?

6. Close your eyes and envision the type of voyage on which you are spending most of your time. Circle the one that best describes your life today.

unanchored   anchored yet wavering   anchored and clinging

7. What adjustments can you make to tighten your grip on the hope of the gospel this week?

8. Ask God to open your eyes to the grace all around you. Envision His powerful, loving hands forever surrounding yours as you learn how to hold fast to hope. Thank Him for this grace.

I am so thankful that I don't have to hold fast to hope on my own. I am weak. You are strong. I am forgetful. You are faithful. I get distracted. You are ever-present. Thank You God, for Your great, great grace.

⁖ BONUS STUDY ⁖

Chose a few verses from our passage to memorize. Write them out on a 3x5 card and post them up around your house in prominent places, to help you remember the truths you've learned this week.

FOCUSING ON **ROMANS** 5:1–5

Hope Is My Harbor

Foundation

FOCUSing ON ROMANS 5:1–5

MY FRIEND LIZ makes everything look good. From her bright red lipstick and blunt-cut bangs to her skinny jeans and heels, she's a woman who can pull just about anything off. She's younger than me, ministers to millennials, and is always up on the latest trends. Every once in a while she uses a term I don't fully understand, and I have to muster up the courage to ask her what she means by it. I'm slowly coming to grips with the fact that I am no longer fresh out of college. She recently had to explain to me what a "baller" is. (Obviously, I'm not one!) Funny thing is, once I learn a new word or phrase from my hip-friend Liz, I see it all around me. Something I never heard of or noticed before is suddenly everywhere.

We've covered a lot of ground over these three short weeks, and I'm excited for this last week of discovering hope together. Maybe you're beginning to see things you've never noticed before when it comes to understanding the gospel-hope you have in Christ. Perhaps the somewhat overwhelming, scholarly terms like justification, sanctification, and glorification are beginning to take shape in your mind's eye. And the "already . . . but not yet" idea of all we have in Christ is beginning to help reconcile what you know is true because of Jesus and what you experience in your everyday?

I truly hope so. I'm praying for you this week, for your view of God to grow continually bigger, for the truths you've learned to penetrate your heart deeper, and for your grip on grace to become increasingly tighter.

1. Open your time in the Word today with a prayer of thankfulness for all God has revealed to you so far. Thank the Spirit for illuminating your way, and Christ for making a way for you to experience hope.

ENJOY EVERY WORD

2. Do your foundation work for Romans 5:1–5 by reading and then writing the passage in whichever way you enjoy.

3. I want you to take one more look at the passage to see if some of the themes we've been studying jump out to you. Specifically, look for the process of our salvation in these verses. In your foundation work above, consider highlighting or underlining the following in separate colors.
• What has happened (justification)
• What is happening (sanctification)
• What will happen (glorification)

The Bible is truly a masterpiece, and the more we learn about these big salvation themes, the more we will see them in detail throughout Scripture. It is through the knowing of these big-picture themes that the Word of God often "comes alive." "The word of God is living and active" (Hebrews 4:12) and incredibly relevant to our everyday moments. I pray you are experiencing these truths more and more each day.

God, I am so thankful for Your Word. It is a gift. Continue Your refining work in me.

⋅!⋅ BONUS STUDY ⋅!⋅

Take some time to read through all or part of the Book of Romans. Pay special attention to the "salvation" themes (justification, sanctification, and glorification) and continue your highlighting work through another passage in Romans.

CHEAT SHEET

3. Look for the process of our salvation in these verses. In your foundation work above, consider highlighting or underlining the following in separate colors.

• **What has happened (justification)**

• <u>What is happening (sanctification)</u>

• *What will happen (glorification)*

> Therefore, since **we have been justified by faith, we have peace with God through our Lord Jesus Christ.** Through him **we have also obtained access by faith into this grace** <u>in which we stand, and we rejoice</u> in *hope of the glory of God.* Not only that, <u>but we rejoice in our sufferings, knowing that suffering produces endurance, and endurance produces character, and character produces hope, and hope does not put us to shame,</u> because **God's love has been poured into our hearts through the Holy Spirit who has been given to us.**
>
> —Romans 5:1–5 ESV

Observation

FOCUSing ON ROMANS 5:1–5

And I heard a loud voice from the throne saying, "Behold, the dwelling place of God is with man. He will dwell with them, and they will be his people, and God himself will be with them as their God."

—Revelation 21:3

THE TRUTHS OF heaven are baffling: pearly gates, golden streets, and a glassy sea. The splendor and beauty of such things are hard to imagine. Often I wonder what it will be like to see loved ones I miss dearly. It's difficult to envision days without experiencing pain, sickness, or tears. And trying to figure out what it will be like to be like Christ and to no longer be stuck in this body of sin? Unfathomable. Yet all these things, though glorious on their own, are nothing compared to the best part about heaven: God.

Many people envision their time in heaven to be spent in the presence of family and lost loved ones, like it will be one long, fabulous dinner party. Perfect fellowship. Perfect food. Perfect family. This is not, however, the biblical portrait of heaven.

"Day and night they never cease to say, 'Holy, holy, holy, is the Lord God Almighty, who was and is and is to come!'" (Revelation 4:8).

God our Father will be at the center of our every heavenly thought, and His glorious presence will be fully experienced and enjoyed for eternity. With both the penalty and presence of sin removed, we will encounter God in ways we simply cannot here on earth. It is this—experiencing God's unhindered power, promises, and peace in every part of our being—we look forward to. Heaven is the harbor in which we will enjoy His glorious presence forever.

1. Take a few moments to imagine what heaven will be like. Consider the incredible glory of God we see here on earth, through blazing, beautiful sunsets, powerful oceans, and captivating mountains. Yet these only display a fraction of God's magnificence. Ask Him to give you a great longing for more of His glorious presence in your life.

LOOK AT THE DETAILS

2. Read Romans 5:1–5 again, and fill out the chart below.

WHAT I POSSESS	WHAT I REJOICE IN

3. Why do you think Paul rejoices in suffering?

4. Look again at Romans 5:1–5, and note what you learn about hope.

TRUTHS ABOUT HOPE

5. Which of these truths stands out to you? Why?

We are limited beings. Our bodies are finite. Our view is obscured. Our understanding is limited. Yet all will live for eternity. If we are in Christ, we will spend our every moment in the glorious presence of our Holy God. And though we don't always understand the hows and the whys of today, we can hold on to the hope that every wave of every storm is allowed for a great purpose, if nothing else, to produce a hope for the unhindered presence of God's glory we will enjoy in heaven.

"For now we see in a mirror dimly, but then face to face. Now I know in part; then I shall know fully, even as I have been fully known" (1 Corinthians 13:12).

God, I believe, help my unbelief! Sometimes the suffering is just too much, and I want to give up, to let go. Thank You for Your grace that continues to hold me. Grant me a fresh confidence in Your goodness, regardless of my circumstances.

⁔ BONUS STUDY ⁔

Compile a master "Hope" list. (See appendix.) Go back through your studies and write out all the truths about hope on one page.

CHEAT SHEET

2. Read Romans 5:1–5 again and fill out the chart below.

WHAT I POSSESS	WHAT I REJOICE IN
• Justification by faith • Peace with God (through Jesus) • Access by faith into grace (through Jesus) • God's love poured into my heart (through the Holy Spirit) • Given the Holy Spirit	• Hope of the glory of God • Sufferings

4. Look again at Romans 5:1–5, and note what you learn about hope.

TRUTHS ABOUT HOPE
Hope in the glory of God Produced by suffering: Suffering → endurance → character → hope My hope in God does not put me to shame

Clarification

FOCUSing ON ROMANS 5:1–5

The Spirit of the Lord God is upon me, because the Lord has anointed me to bring good news . . . that they may be called oaks of righteousness, the planting of the Lord, that he may be glorified.

—ISAIAH 61:1–3

TREE-SHAPING—THE PRACTICE of using living trees to create art—is not very prevalent here in the United States, but I saw many of these "arborsculptures" in China. We spent six weeks in East Asia and often sighted very unusually shaped trees. To make them, the artists carefully form, guide, and monitor a tree's growth to produce an artistic structure. From an impressive geometric latticework to a beautiful chair shape, many different structures can be created. Much time, commitment, and patience is needed to achieve the desired forms, as most of these structures take well over a decade of growth, careful training, and a clear vision of the final product.

In John 15, we are given the picture of our Father God as the vinedresser who lovingly prunes the vine to produce more fruit. Ephesians 2:10 tells us that we are God's workmanship. You and I are each a masterpiece of God, created and prepared for a good work. Our "already . . . but not yet" time here on earth is intentional. If we existed solely to experience our own salvation, I believe God would take us up into heaven at the moment of our salvation. But He doesn't, and the Bible is clear that you and I live another day for a great purpose.

We are "oaks of righteousness," planted by God for His glory. He is carefully and intentionally shaping us into a masterpiece, and we are to long for the day that His work in us will be complete. This process is not easy, nor does it come without difficulty and endurance. Pruning is painful, but if we can learn to see our sufferings as an avenue to hope, we too can rejoice in adversity. Because suffering produces a strong endurance, which produces deep character, which produces an unshakeable hope in all of God's promises.

1. What sufferings are you currently facing? Spend some time journaling out all that is heavy on your heart. Ask God to give you perspective on how these ugly hardships are actually bringing out beauty in your life. Declare your desire for Him to be glorified in you through your sufferings.

UNCOVER THE ORIGINAL MEANING

Spend some time today discovering the original language. I've given a few suggestions of what to study but, as always, feel free to follow your own inclinations of which word to look up. If the Greek is still too overwhelming, simply choose a few words to look up in the dictionary and write out their definitions.

Step 1: DECIDE which English word you would like to study.
Read Romans 5:1–5. As you find any repeated word or words that seem important to the passage, write them down.

Step 2: DISCOVER the Greek word in an interlinear Bible.

Together, let's focus on the word *produces*. Using an interlinear Bible, find the original word for *produces* used in verses 3 and 4 and write it below. Your version might use *develop*, *brings about*, or *work*.

produces =

Step 3: DEFINE that Greek word using a Greek lexicon.

Now, look up the Greek word you've uncovered in a lexicon and note the following:

Lexicon discovery:

• Definition:

• Times used:

• Part of speech:

• Other ways it is translated:

• Any special notes:

2. Follow the above steps to look up one more word. Here are a few words to choose from:

Sufferings (v. 3)

Endurance (vv. 3, 4)

Character (v. 4)

Lexicon discovery:

• Definition:

• Times used:

• Part of speech:

• Other ways it is translated:

• Any special notes:

3. What discoveries did you make through your clarification study? Which word did you learn the most about?

God has a clear vision and purpose for my life, and He is continually growing, shaping, and pruning me to become the masterpiece I was born to become. Yet, this molding does not come without pain, nor does it happen without the hard work and patience of my own as I cling to God's goodness in the midst of the bending. This week's passage gives us a glimpse of how our loving vinedresser uses every difficulty in our lives to produce in us a blazing and beautiful display of God's glory, producing a steady and firm grasp on our hope to come.

"For I consider that the sufferings of this present time are not worth comparing with the glory that is to be revealed to us" (Romans 8:18).

> God, grant me the ability to see life through the eyes of eternity. Use the sufferings I face to loosen my grip on the things of this world, and tighten my grasp on the hope I have in You alone. Thank You for lovingly, patiently, and carefully pruning me to become a brighter display of Your glory.

⁖ BONUS STUDY ⁖

Look up additional words throughout each verse in this week's passage.

CHEAT SHEET

Step 3: DEFINE that Greek word using a Greek lexicon.

Produces = katergazomai

Lexicon discovery: katergazomai

- Definition: accomplish, prepare
- Times used: 22
- Part of speech: verb
- Other ways it is translated: work, do, prepare, accomplish, bring about, carry
- Any special notes: Strong's #G2716

Utilization

FOCUSing ON ROMANS 5:1–5

For I consider that the sufferings of this present time are not worth comparing with the glory that is to be revealed to us.

—ROMANS 8:18

MY SUPER-COOL FRIEND Liz—the one with the bright red lipstick and hip phrases—has been on her own journey of hope as she and her husband await to complete their family through international adoption. For half a decade now, they have sought out and fought hard to bring home a sibling group from various countries in Africa. Twice they have been on the homestretch, ready to complete their journey. Twice they have had to start from scratch. Today they stand, awaiting a final match with a sibling group from Burundi.

In Liz's heart, these children are hers. She prays for them. She loves them. They are a part of her. Already . . . but not yet. There are legalities remaining and more periods of waiting. But with every exciting step forward and disappointing setback, she experiences the realities of Romans 5:1–5. This long, suffering wait produces a strong endurance, which produces strong character, which produces a strong hope for the day she will walk into that orphanage, sweep her beloved babies up into her arms and bring them to their forever home. With every day that passes, her longing for them grows.

The longing is great because the wait has been long.

I imagine those sweet souls walking the dusty streets of Burundi and hope for their own safe harbor; longing for the day when their mother and father will arrive, arms open, ready to take them home to their forever family. You and I are like those precious, chosen little ones. Adopted. Brought into the family of God, already . . . but not yet. We too await our forever home, clinging to the hope we have in Jesus who has provided a way to our safe harbor where God will sweep us up into His presence for eternity.

I'm praying today that God would overwhelm you with the truth of His forever love for you. You are adopted. Chosen. Loved. Cherished. And this world? It's not our home, but a mere shadow of eternity, and the joys we experience here pale in comparison to the majesty we will experience in God's presence in heaven . . . for eternity.

1. Take an objective look at your life and where you tend to find "safe harbor." In other words: where do you run for comfort, safety, and joy as you await the fullness of His forever presence? Ask God to give you a greater vision for the hope you have in Christ, and thus a greater longing for your true and lasting safe harbor.

DISCOVER THE CONNECTIONS

Yesterday we looked at the Greek word *katergazomai* together and learned this word can be translated into many different English words (*work, do, prepare, accomplish, bring about, carry*), giving us a deeper understanding of the author's true meaning of the word. For our utilization study today, all of our cross-references contain this word *katergazomai*.

2. Read Romans 5:1–5 one more time to start your study today.

Read each reference below and look for truths about what is being produced (katergazomai) in us. Write out your observations in the charts provided. (Hint: *katergazomai* is contained in the verse noted in parentheses.)

James 1:2–4 (See v. 3.)

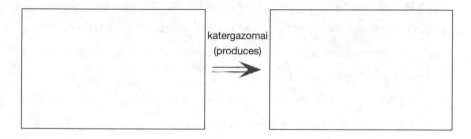

2 Corinthians 4:16–18 (See v. 17.)

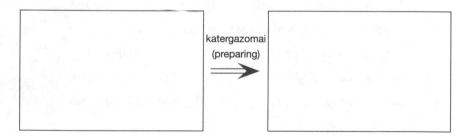

Philippians 2:12–13 (See v. 12.)

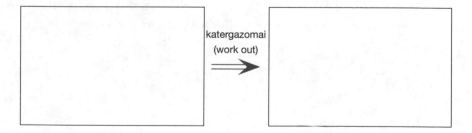

I don't claim to understand the whys behind every trial in my life or yours, but this I do believe with all my heart: God is good. God is loving. God is ever-present, even in my darkest of days. He makes good come from every evil. At the least, every trial, burden, and evil we encounter is good because it points us to the glorious hope we have in the safe harbor of God's forever presence. And it is from this firm foundation we work out our salvation, we allow the katergazomai production, the sanctifying power of suffering build up endurance, then character, then hope. We accomplish the hard work of holding on to hope, regardless of the waves that try to beat us down.

"And we know that for those who love God all things work together for good, for those who are called according to his purpose" (Romans 8:28).

God, thank You for choosing me and adopting me. I praise You for the difficult seasons. Help me cling to hope, especially during the storms of life. Open my eyes more and more to the truths about all I have to look forward to in eternity with You. Make my heart to long for eternity more and more each day.

⫶ BONUS STUDY ⫶

Read each of today's passages and write out all the commands given.

Look up cross-referencing for additional phrases in each verse in this week's passage.

CHEAT SHEET

2. Read Romans 5:1–5 one more time to start your study today. Read each reference below and look for truths about what is being produced (katergazomai) in us. Write out your observations in the charts provided. (Hint: katergazomai is contained in the verse noted in parentheses.)

James 1:2–4 (See v. 3.)

meet trials of various kinds; testing of your faith	katergazomai (produces)	full effect of steadfastness; perfect and complete, lacking in nothing

2 Corinthians 4:16–18 (See v. 17.)

light momentary affliction	katergazomai (preparing)	eternal weight of glory beyond all comparison

Philippians 2:12-13 (See v. 12.)

obey; fear and trembling; God's work in me (salvation) enables me	katergazomai (work out)	His good pleasure

Summation

FOCUSing ON ROMANS 5:1–5

In Christ alone my hope is found.

—Keith Getty

THE HOPE OF the gospel is our treasure. A gift, granted freely by grace to all who would draw near to God through faith. Once it is in our possession it can never be lost, corrupted, or taken away from us.

The hope of the gospel is our lighthouse. Our shining beacon, guiding and protecting us as we fight every day to remember the truth about all we have through Christ.

The hope of the gospel is our anchor. Our steadfast tether for the storms of life. As we learn to keep a tight grip on our anchor, we experience the moment-by-moment presence of God's grace in our everyday life.

The hope of the gospel is our harbor. Our final, eternal destination where we will experience the unhindered, glorious presence of God and the fulfillment of every promise in Christ.

All this, by the work of Christ. Jesus, who humbled Himself and came to earth to live a perfect life, so that He could be the spotless sacrifice needed to set us free from the bondage of sin and give us a glorious future. Our Savior, who was brutally killed, buried in a tomb, and rose again to bring power over death, now resides in us. The very presence of God dwells with us, in our everyday, bringing abundant, hope-filled life as we wait to meet Him face-to-face.

What a great hope we have in Jesus!

"To them God chose to make known how great among the Gentiles are the riches of the glory of this mystery, which is Christ in you, the hope of glory" (Colossians 1:27).

1. Spend a few moments in praise of all you have, through Christ. Thank God for the hope you have been given, the hope you have to cling to now, and the hope of all that is to come.

RESPOND TO GOD'S WORD

IDENTIFY: What's the main idea?
Take a few moments to flip back to each day of this week's study to review what you've learned.

2. Write out Romans 5:1–5 in your own words.

3. Read a commentary or study Bible to see how your observations line up. As you search the commentaries, ask God to make clear the meaning of any passages that are fuzzy to you. Record any additional observations.

If you still have any lingering questions about this week's verse, ask a trusted pastor, mentor, or friend what they think about the verse, or enter the online discussion at BibleStudyHub.com.

MODIFY: How do my beliefs line up to this main idea?

4. How does your view of suffering line up with what you've learned this week?

5. How does your view of heaven line up with what you've learned this week?

6. When you navigate through the storms of life, do you tend to cling to the hope of our steadfast God, or are you looking for rescue and comfort from people or the temporary provisions of this world?

GLORIFY: In light of this main idea, how can I realign my life to best reflect God's glory?

7. What adjustments can you make to tighten your grip on the hope of heaven as you endure hardships?

8. Spend time in honest prayer, asking God to uncover the places in your heart that are clinging to something other than the hope you have in Jesus. Declare your utter need for grace to hold fast today, tomorrow, and for a lifetime.

Father God, I am overcome by Your great love for me. Jesus, I am humbled by Your example and sacrifice. Holy Spirit, I am thankful and in desperate need for Your enabling grace to endure the seasons of life ahead of me. Help me. Hold me. Guide me. Sustain me. Grant my heart an insatiable desire for Your forever, unhindered presence, and may this drive me to continue journeying closer and closer to Your loving, safe harbor.

⁙ BONUS STUDY ⁙

Chose a few verses from our passage to memorize. Write them out on a 3x5 card, and post them up around your house in prominent places to help you remember the truths you've learned this week.

Appendix

A Note from Katie

Thank you for taking this journey through *Everyday Hope* with me. My prayer is that you stand today with a greater grasp on the gospel-hope you have in Jesus, and a practical understanding on how you can experience everyday, moment-by-moment hope—regardless of circumstances. Everyday hope is found by holding fast, by remembering all that is true of the capable God who loves you and has given you great and precious promises to cling to as you await the fullness of His forever presence in heaven.

The glorious, gracious gospel of Jesus is good news. Let's hold fast to it.

Glossary of Bible Study Terms

Interlinear Bible: a translation where each English word is linked to its original Greek word. There are many free interlinear Bibles online, as well as great apps you can download to your phone or tablet. Check out KatieOrr.me/Resources for current links.

Concordance: a helpful list of words found in the original languages of the Bible (mainly Hebrew and Greek) and the verses where you can find them.

Cross-reference: a notation in a Bible verse that indicates there are other passages that contain similar material.

Footnote: a numerical notation that refers readers to the bottom of a page for additional information.

Commentary: a reference book written by experts that explains the Bible. A good commentary will give you historical background and language information that may not be obvious from the passage.

Greek: the language in which most of the New Testament was written.

Hebrew: the language in which most of the Old Testament was written

Structure and Books of the Bible

Books of the Law (also
known as the Pentateuch)

  Genesis

  Exodus

  Leviticus

  Numbers

  Deuteronomy

Books of History

  Joshua

  Judges

  Ruth

  1 Samuel

  2 Samuel

  1 Kings

  2 Kings

  1 Chronicles

  2 Chronicles

  Ezra

  Nehemiah

  Esther

Wisdom Literature

  Job

  Psalms

  Proverbs

  Ecclesiastes

  Song of Songs

Major Prophets

  Isaiah

  Jeremiah

  Lamentations

  Ezekiel

  Daniel

Minor Prophets

  Hosea

  Joel

  Amos

  Obadiah

  Jonah

  Micah

  Nahum

  Habakkuk

  Zephaniah

  Haggai

  Zechariah

  Malachi

New Testament (First four together are known as "The Gospels")

- Matthew
- Mark
- Luke
- John
- Acts

Epistles (or Letters) by Paul

- Romans
- 1 Corinthians
- 2 Corinthians
- Galatians
- Ephesians
- Philippians
- Colossians
- 1 Thessalonians
- 2 Thessalonians

1 Timothy
2 Timothy
Titus
Philemon

General Epistles (Letters not by Paul)

- Hebrews
- James
- 1 Peter
- 2 Peter
- 1 John
- 2 John
- 3 John
- Jude

Apocalyptic Writing

- Revelation

Major Themes of the Bible

Though many view Scripture as a patchwork of historical accounts, morality tales, and wisdom for daily living, the Bible is really only one story—the mind-blowing story of God's plan to rescue fallen humanity. This storyline flows through every single book, chapter, verse, and word of Scripture. It's crucial that we know the movements, or themes, of the grand storyline so we don't miss the point of the passage we are studying.

For example, I grew up hearing about the story of David's adulterous affair with the beautiful, but married, Bathsheba. I heard how he covered his misdeeds with a murderous plot to snuff out her husband. This story was usually punctuated with a moral that went something like this, "Don't take what isn't yours!" While it is indeed good practice to refrain from taking what isn't ours, there is a much bigger connection to the grand story that we will miss if we stop at a moral lesson. So what then is this grand story, and how can we recognize it?

The story falls into four main themes, or movements: creation, fall, redemption, and completion*.

CREATION

The Bible begins by describing the creative work of God. His masterwork and crowning achievement was the creation of people. God put the first couple, Adam and Eve, in absolute paradise and gave them everything they needed to thrive. The best part of this place, the Garden of Eden, was that God walked among His people. They knew Him and were known by Him. The Bible even says they walked around naked because they had no concept of shame or guilt. (See Genesis 2:25.) Life was perfect, just like God had designed.

FALL

In the Garden, God provided everything for Adam and Eve. But He also gave them instructions for how to live and established boundaries for their protection. Eventually, the first family decided to cross the boundary, and break the one rule God commanded them to keep. This decision was the most fateful error in history. At that precise moment, paradise was lost. The connection people experienced with God vanished. Adam and Eve's act was not simply a mistake but outright rebellion against the sovereign creator of the universe. It was, in no uncertain terms, a declaration of war against God. Every aspect of creation was fractured in that moment. Because of their choice, Adam and Eve introduced death and disease to the world, but more importantly, put a chasm between mankind and God that neither Adam nor Eve nor any person could ever hope to cross. Ever since the fall, all people are born with a tendency to sin. Like moths to a light, we are drawn to sin, and like Adam and Eve, our sin pushes us further away from any hope of experiencing God. You see God cannot be good if he doesn't punish sin, but if we all receive the punishment our sin deserves we would all be cast away from Him forever.

REDEMPTION

Fortunately, God was not caught off guard when Adam and Eve rebelled. God knew they would and had a plan in place to fix what they had broken. This plan meant sending Jesus to earth. Even though Jesus was the rightful King of all creation, He came to earth in perfect humility. He walked the earth for more than 30 years experiencing everything you and I do. Jesus grew tired at the end of a long day. He got hungry when He didn't eat. He felt the pain of losing loved ones, and the disappointment of betrayal from friends. He went through all of life like we do with one massive exception—He never sinned. Jesus never disobeyed God, not even once. Because He was without sin, He was the only one in history who could bridge the gap between God and us. However, redemption came at a steep price. Jesus was nailed to a wooden cross and left to die a criminal's death. While He hung on the Cross God put the full weight of our sin upon Jesus. When the King of the universe died, He paid the penalty for our sin. God poured out His righteous anger toward our sin on the sinless One. After Jesus died, He was buried and many believed all hope was lost. However, Jesus did not stay dead—having defeated sin on the Cross, He was raised from death and is alive today!

COMPLETION

The final theme in the grand storyline of the Bible is completion, the end of the story. Now that Jesus has paid the penalty for our sin, we have hope of reconciliation with God. This is such tremendous news because reconciliation means we are forgiven of sin and given eternal life. Reconciliation means that God dwells with us again. Finally, we know Him and are known by Him. Completion for us means entering into reconciliation with God through the only means He provided. We can only experience reconciliation under God's rescue plan if we trust Jesus to pay for our sin, and demonstrate this by repenting, or turning away, from our sin. But God's rescue plan does not end with us. One day, Jesus will come back and ultimately fix every part of fallen creation. King Jesus will come back to rule over God's people, and again establish a paradise that is free from the effects of sin.

Let's return to the David and Bathsheba story for a moment and try to find our place. David was the greatest, most godly king in the history of the Old Testament, but even he was affected by the fall and had a sinful nature. This story points out that what we really need is not a more disciplined eye, but a total transformation. We need to be delivered from the effects of the fall. It also illustrates how we don't simply need a king who loves God, but we need a King who is God. Do you see how this story connects to the arc of the grand storyline? Just look at how much glorious truth we miss out on if we stop short at "don't take what isn't yours."

*For a more detailed discussion on these themes, refer to Part 1 and 2 of *The Explicit Gospel* by Matt Chandler (pages 21–175) or Chapter 2 of Mark Dever's *The Gospel and Personal Evangelism* (pages 31–44).

Understanding the Ceremonial Law

TENT/TABERNACLE

WHAT IT WAS: The Tabernacle, or Tent of Meeting, was a portable sanctuary that served as the location of God's dwelling place on earth before the Temple was built. Craftsmen built the Tabernacle during the period of the Exodus when the Israelites wandered in the wilderness after leaving Egypt and before entering the Promised Land. During the Israelite's desert wanderings, the Tabernacle was situated in the center of the encampment.

ITS IMPORTANCE: The Tabernacle was a portable place of worship for the Israelites, allowing it to be moved as the camp moved.

NEW TESTAMENT SIGNIFICANCE: In the New Testament, God's presence dwells in each Christian.

KEY PASSAGES: Exodus 26; Numbers 1:51; 2:17; 18:21–24

TEMPLE

WHAT IT WAS: A permanent building that was the center of Hebrew worship. The original Temple was built by Solomon in 960 BC and took the place of the Tabernacle. The Temple was destroyed in AD 70 and has not been rebuilt.

ITS IMPORTANCE: The Temple was the dwelling place of God's presence on earth. The Temple was also to be the place where people from all nations could come and experience the one true God.

NEW TESTAMENT SIGNIFICANCE: In the New Testament, God's presence dwells in each Christian.

KEY PASSAGES: 2 Samuel 7:2–16; 1 Kings 5; 6; 8; 1 Corinthians 6:19; Ephesians 2:9–22

HOLY OF HOLIES

WHAT IT WAS: The inner sanctuary of the Temple (and before that, the inner sanctuary of the Tabernacle) contained the Ark of the Covenant. This room was separated from the rest of the Temple (or Tabernacle) by a large curtain called the veil.

ITS IMPORTANCE: This was the location where the sacrifice for Israel's sin was to be made on the Day of Atonement. The penalty for entering this room in an inappropriate way was death.

NEW TESTAMENT SIGNIFICANCE: Immediately following Jesus' death, the curtain separating the Holy of Holies was torn from top to bottom. There is nothing separating believers from God's presence.

KEY PASSAGES: Leviticus 16; Matthew 27:50–51

PRIESTS

WHAT THEY WERE: Professional ministers who performed ceremonial tasks in the service of God. Priests could only come from the tribe of

Levi, and had to be a direct descendent of Aaron, the brother of Moses.

THEIR IMPORTANCE: Only priests could perform the tasks of ceremonial worship.

NEW TESTAMENT SIGNIFICANCE: All believers have direct access to God, and are themselves priests.

KEY PASSAGES: Leviticus 8–10; 1 Timothy 2:5; 1 Peter 2:4–9

HIGH PRIESTS

WHAT THEY WERE: The High Priest was the highest ranking priest in Hebrew culture.

THEIR IMPORTANCE: The High Priest was the only priest who could enter the Holy of Holies on the Day of Atonement.

NEW TESTAMENT SIGNIFICANCE: Jesus is the Great High Priest who made a once and final sacrifice for our sin.

KEY PASSAGES: Hebrews 4:14–16; 10:1–18

ATONEMENT

WHAT IT WAS: Atonement is the necessary action required to remove the penalty of sin. In the Old Testament, atonement for sin required the blood sacrifice of an unblemished animal. Once a year, on the Day of Atonement, the High Priest makes a sacrifice on behalf of all Israel. During that sacrifice, one ram is killed to cover Israel's sin, and another is led into the wilderness to remove Israel's sin.

ITS IMPORTANCE: Sin always requires the shedding of blood. When Adam and Eve sinned, their nakedness was made known. To cover them, God killed an animal. In order to cover the sin of an entire people, God instituted the ceremonial law and the Day of Atonement. Atonement enforces God's justice while maintaining His mercy.

NEW TESTAMENT SIGNIFICANCE: Jesus is the spotless lamb who both covers our sin and removes it from our lives. Jesus' death is the final atonement that will be made for the sin of mankind, and thus fulfills the ceremonial law.

KEY PASSAGES: Leviticus 16; Hebrews 10:1–18; 1 Peter 1:19

How to Do a Greek Word Study

Learning more about the language used in the original version of Scripture can be a helpful tool toward a better understanding of the author's original meaning and intention in writing.

STEP 1: DECIDE which English word you would like to study.
Do a quick read of your passage and note any potential keywords and/or repeated words. There is no right or wrong way to do this! Simply select a few words you would like to learn more about.

STEP 2: DISCOVER the Greek word in an interlinear Bible.
Using an interlinear Bible (see glossary), find the original Greek word for each instance of the word in the passage you are studying. There may be more than one Greek word present.

STEP 3: DEFINE the Greek word using a Greek lexicon.
Look up your Greek word (or words if you found more than one) in a Greek lexicon (see glossary).

Continue through these three steps for each word you would like to study.

Truths About Hope Master Sheet

Use this space to record all truths discovered about hope.

TRUTHS ABOUT HOPE

The Good News

GOD LOVES YOU

You are known and deeply loved by a great, glorious, and personal God. This God hand-formed you for a purpose (Ephesians 2:10), He has called you by name (Isaiah 43:1) and you are of great worth to Him (Luke 12:6–7).

WE HAVE A SIN PROBLEM

We are all sinners and are all therefore separated from God (Romans 3:23; 6:23). Even the "smallest" of sins is a great offense to God. He is a righteous judge who will not be in the presence of sin, and cannot allow sin to go unpunished. Our natural tendency toward sin has left us in desperate need of rescue because God must deal with our sin.

JESUS IS THE ONLY SOLUTION

Since God's standard is perfection, and we have all fallen short of the mark, Jesus is the *only* answer to our sin problem (John 14:6). Jesus lived a life of perfect obedience to God. So when Jesus died on the Cross, He alone was able to pay the penalty of our sin. After His death, Jesus rose from the dead, defeating death, and providing the one way we could be reconciled to God (2 Corinthians 5:17–21). Jesus Christ is the only one who can save us from our sins.

WE MUST CHOOSE TO BELIEVE

Trusting Christ is our only part in the gospel. Specifically, the Bible requires us to have faith in what Christ has done on our behalf (Ephesians 2:8–9). This type of faith is not just belief in God. Many people grow up believing that God exists but never enter into the Christian faith. Faith that saves comes from a desperate heart. A heart that longs for Jesus— the only solution for their sin problem—to be first and foremost in their life. We demonstrate that we have this type of saving faith by turning away, or repenting, from our sin.

FOCUSed 15 Study Method

APPLY THIS METHOD to 2–10 verses a day, over a week's time, for a deep encounter with God through His Word, in as little as 15 minutes a day.

Foundation: Enjoy Every Word
Read and rewrite the passage—Summarize, draw pictures, sentence-diagram, or simply copy the passage. Do whatever helps you slow down and enjoy each word.

Observation: Look at the Details
Take notes on what you see—Write down what is true in this passage. Look for truths about the character of God, promises to cling to, or commands given.

Clarification: Uncover the Original Meaning
- Decide which English word to study.
- Discover the Hebrew word in an interlinear Bible.
- Define that Hebrew word using a Hebrew lexicon.

Utilization: Discover the Connections in Scripture
Cross-reference—Look up the references in each verse to view the threads and themes throughout the Bible.

Summation: Respond to God's Word

- Identify the main idea of each passage.

- Modify my beliefs to the truths found in this passage.

- Glorify God by aligning my life to reflect the truths I've discovered.

New Hope® Publishers is a division of WMU®, an international organization that challenges Christian believers to understand and be radically involved in God's mission. For more information about WMU, go to wmu.com. More information about New Hope books may be found at NewHopePublishers.com. New Hope books may be purchased at your local bookstore.

Use the QR reader on your smartphone to visit us online at NewHopePublishers.com

If you've been blessed by this book, we would like to hear your story. The publisher and author welcome your comments and suggestions at: newhopereader@wmu.org.

Also in the FOCUSed 15 series

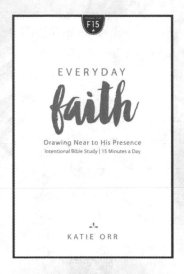

ISBN-13: 978-1-59669-461-3
N164101 · $11.99

What does real faith look like?

Everyday Faith, an easy-to-use, four-week study, helps you find out how to draw near to God's presence in as few as 15 minutes, five days a week. Designed for women who are pressed for time but crave depth from their Bible study, *Everyday Faith* utilizes the FOCUSed 15 method, which values quality above quantity.

As it guides you through the Book of Hebrews, you will discover truths, promises, and commands; uncover word meanings; and discover your part in God's plan.

For more information, visit NewHopePublishers.com
and preview a video of Katie as she walks readers through
the FOCUS study method!

Also in the FOCUSed15 series

ISBN-13: 978-1-59669-463-7
N164103 · $11.99

What does Christian love look like in everyday moments?

Everyday Love—an easy-to-use, four-week study—helps you discover how your life can daily bear witness to God's purpose. Designed for women who are pressed for time but crave depth from their Bible study, *Everyday Love* utilizes the FOCUS method, which values quality over quantity and takes as few as 15 minutes a day.

This study guides you through 1 Corinthians 13 so you can find truths, promises, and commands; uncover word meanings; and discover your part in God's plan.

For more information, visit NewHopePublishers.com
and preview a video of Katie as she walks readers through
the FOCUS study method!

WorldCrafts℠ develops sustainable,
fair-trade businesses among impoverished
people around the world.

Each WorldCrafts product represents lives changed
by the opportunity to earn an income with
dignity and to hear the offer of everlasting life.

Visit NewHopePublishers.com/FOCUSed15
to shop WorldCrafts products related to the
FOCUSed15 Bible study series!

WORLDCRAFTS℠
Committed. Holistic. Fair Trade.
WorldCrafts.org 1-800-968-7301